BORN APART, BECOMING ONE

BORN APART, BECOMING ONE

Disciples Defeating Racism

WILLIAM CHRIS HOBGOOD

CHALICE
PRESS

ST. LOUIS, MISSOURI

Bible quotations, unless otherwise noted, are from the *New Revised Standard Version Bible,* copyright 1989, Division of Christian Education of the National Council of the Churches of Christ in the United States of America. Used by permission. All rights reserved.

The poem on page 84, "A just anger," from CIRCLES ON THE WATER by Marge Piercy, copyright ©1982 by Marge Piercy. Used by permission of Alfred A. Knopf, a division of Random House, Inc. All rights reserved.

Cover image: FotoSearch
Cover and interior design: Elizabeth Wright

Visit Chalice Press on the World Wide Web at
www.chalicepress.com

10 9 8 7 6 5 4 3 2 1   09 10 11 12 13 14 15 16

Library of Congress Cataloging–in–Publication Data

Hobgood, William Chris.
  Born apart, becoming one : Disciples defeating racism / William Chris Hobgood.
    p. cm.
  ISBN 978-0-8272-0239-9
  1. Race relations—Religious aspects—Christian Churches (Disciples of Christ) I. Title.

BX7321.3.H63 2009
286.6'3—dc22

                                             2008044134

Contents

Introduction

The purpose of this book is to enable a deep exploration of the relationship of the Christian Church (Disciples of Christ) to the pro-reconciliation/anti-racism initiative of our denomination, with the goal of engaging individuals and congregations in this initiative to dismantle institutional racism. A colleague said to me, "Your passion is anti-racism; mine is the vitalization of congregations." My response is congregations cannot experience vitalization in the twenty-first century without engaging racism. Racism is still active. It will never stop its insidious work just because we'd like it to.

The book divides in three sections: (1) a brief examination of Disciples of Christ history, particularly as it relates to the racism that was already doing its work in the U.S.A. when we were born; (2) a look at several core elements that have been part of our life from the beginning and that offer places for important anti-racism work to be done; and (3) ways to move ahead in the battle against racism. All of this is couched in the framework of our larger grounding as God's people and as part of the church of Jesus Christ.

Several colleagues need to be named. My partners in the work as core organizers/trainers for the Christian Church (Disciples of Christ) are Jessica Vázquez, Martha Herrin, and Marcus Leathers. I am grateful to them for their passion. They are amazing team members and teachers. Several organizer/trainers from Crossroads Anti-racism have been vital partners as we four learned our way into this deep area. Our church is deeply indebted to that organization.

A host of committed Disciples have become part of this movement. We have many regional teams and more to come. Some people are terribly hurt and deeply offended by racism's grip. I am grateful to them and in awe of the amazing patience and impatience of so many.

A particular note of thanks is, finally, saved for two people. Cary Meade Hobgood has been most patient with me as I tested ideas, struggled with times when the right words wouldn't come, fumed at the computer for its tricks, and then got something together. And then there is my dear friend and colleague, Brenda Cardwell. She has taught me so much, more with example than words, though she can sure say the words when we she has to. It was Brenda, though, whose passion really engaged me in what is now my lifelong struggle against the evil of racism.

It has been said time and again that racism will not be overcome until white persons move to confess and then share privilege. But we white persons cannot do this without the support, care, and partnership of persons of color who love God and Jesus Christ and who, for reasons I sometimes cannot understand, still love us.

CHAPTER 1

A Spiritual Movement Begins on the Frontier

Freedom: this was the word. It was more than a word, though. From the beginning it was at the core of the driving spirit that led to the birth and formation of the Stone and Campbell movements. These emerged and converged on the American frontier early in the nineteenth century. Beginning in frontier "sacramental meetings" to celebrate the Lord's Supper, great revivals came about, climaxing in August 1801 at Cane Ridge, where Barton Warren Stone was pastor. This movement was, in many ways, a frontier celebration of religious freedom.

This is not to suggest that all that the revival participants or frontier Disciples did was joyous. It does, though, affirm the truth that much of their life together was lived out in the knowledge that God had given each of them the intellect and spirit to be a free thinker. They joined in congregations and larger fellowships without the necessity of overarching creeds and confessions. The simple confession of faith in Jesus as the Christ was all they asked of people who sought out this fresh way. In this simplicity was a new degree of happiness of spirit, not often found in some of the somber faith expressions that had been around for various lengths of time. Some historians have said that post-revolutionary America pitted Calvinism with its gloomy way of life against the freedom that had been won and was so cherished. "People intent on breaking the expansive designs of moderate Calvinists could do so in the name of extreme liberty or extreme dependence on primitive models."[1] For many the Stone-Campbell Movement was that freedom lived in the practice of faith.

The Disciples as a Spiritual People

One way of understanding spirituality is that it is the place where what is "heard" from God meets our daily lives and makes a difference in the ways we make decisions and then act.[2] Spirituality is where God's guidance and our lives intersect and as a result our lives are never the same again. Using this understanding, we can affirm that the Disciples Movement has a spirituality of freedom in Christ.

That freedom awareness certainly changed the ways people acted. It surely transformed lives and life together. The spiritual base of the Stone-Campbell Movement can be found in a conviction that individual believers could be in personal and direct "touch" with God, needing no intervening person, whether priest or saint in eternity, to be there on their behalf.

One of the great liabilities of this understanding was that faith could be treated as simply a personal faith process, for no longer did creeds and the other formulations of human-centered councils prevail as doctrinal truth. Now I, even as a frontier commoner with little education, could be my own priest and, if asked, priest to someone else. On the other hand, this same Movement found strength in the power of a community of faith formed, not because of rules and articles imposed externally, perhaps long ago, but simply because people chose, or felt called, to be there.

It was in this way that the early leaders found a great opening for reuniting the fractured body of Christ. When Barton Stone said, as he probably did many times, "Let the love of unity be our polar star,"[3] he was not just offering a catchy slogan to get attention. Stone was giving voice to the greatest yearning of his fellow faith-followers: the passion to gather people together in a faith-based freedom and thus transcend the walls that humans had formed to divide people who follow God and Jesus Christ.

In a sense, the Stone-Campbell Movement was institutionalized "down-to-earthness." It was as though on the frontier a decent, freedom-loving, somewhat self-confident, rational way of being needed a spiritual home. This simple, oppression-resisting, honest way of living yearned, or so it appeared, to be rooted in more than just daily survival. A lot of people were like this. Inspired by their migrations westward to carve out new lives for themselves, many found a spiritual home in this new church, a church no longer dependent on the economics of the old colonies. The new church was, like them, young, at least in spirit, and vibrant with freedom.

The question was: can God "organize" these people into something called a *church*? When some had been offended and even rejected by *church* in the past, would they come to a *church* now? What would its purpose be? In time would there be a tipping point from being a reflection of the way people are to a shaper of the way people can be?

The same questions can be asked in 2008. How does all of this coalesce into a process of combating racism? The openness of frontier people to this new Movement made it a very natural and fertile field for new understandings of how to live. Freedom of faith and person could quite naturally be expanded into an understanding of freedom as God's gift to all creation. Combating racism is certainly a struggle whose time has more than come. In truth, it is long overdue and this Movement's love of freedom and passion for the worth of each person make this a place where this combat against racism must be waged. But, to avoid getting too far ahead of where we need to be, we return to the growth of the Disciples of the Stone-Campbell Movement.

I am a "cradle" Disciple of Christ, born this way and committed to being one all of my days. However, many among us came from other places. The congregation of which my spouse and I are part is made up of folks from all walks of faith, with some two thirds being non-Disciple in background. All found this home because of the simplicity of worship, the love and mutual support within the congregation, active ministries in the larger community, and the lack of complex theological trimmings and required beliefs. For many the weekly Lord's Supper, with its administration shared by lay and clergy, was an appealing event. Years ago the Disciples of Christ were called, by Lyle Schaller (an expert on church dynamics), a "bridge church," where people from various places could find a welcoming home.

Our Frontier Roots and Character

Our history, in retrospect, is most predictable. We came to life on the new frontier, west of the Allegheny Mountains, in days when those frontier settlers were relishing their new freedom. We were part of a religious counterpart to the political/economic freedom movement that was sweeping the land. Organized simply, with no complex beliefs required of participants, we placed the emphasis on the individual's right, tools, and responsibility to shape his or her faith. The leaders of the church were expected to say what they believed, but their beliefs were not required of others.

Alexander Campbell, our longest-lived and most noted founder (1788–1866), carried on a near lifelong dialogue with the frontier inhabitants and the developing nation, much of it through his writings: first in the Christian Baptist then in the Millennial Harbinger. In both he often stated his opinions on matters of faith and theology. Campbell was no shallow thinker. He was opinionated, brilliant, and articulate, but always knew that he was not giving voice to a formal doctrinal position of the church; rather, he was taking a lead role in the shaping of a movement. He believed this movement could not live unless people used reason. God did not gift people with reason just so that they could figure out how to check their brains at the door of the church. He was also an educator, first through the Buffalo Seminary and then in Bethany College, founded by him in 1840 and still thriving. It is estimated that Disciples formed over 400 institutions of learning in the nineteenth century.[4] In many ways, Mr. Campbell's experience is the model for Disciples growth and evolution over the years, both during and since his time.

Campbell's approach to the Bible reflects his deep commitment to reason. His was an early version of form criticism, all the more remarkable because he predated many of the scientific discoveries, such as Darwin's work, which contributed method, if not belief, to biblical studies. An abbreviated version of Campbell's rules for biblical interpretation looks like this:

Rule I. On opening any book in the sacred scriptures, consider first the historical circumstances of the book. These are the order, the title, the author, the date, the place, and the occasion of it.

II. In examining the contents of any book, as respects precepts, promises, exhortations, etc., observe who it is that speaks, and under what dispensation he officiates. Is he a Patriarch, a Jew, or a Christian? Consider also the persons he addressed—their prejudices, characters, and religious relations.

III. To understand the meaning of what is commanded, promised, taught, etc., the same philological principles, deduced from the nature of language, or the same laws of interpretation which are applied to the language of other books, are to be applied to the language of the Bible.

IV. Common usage...must always decide the meaning of any word which has but one signification; but when words have according to...the Dictionary more meanings than one, whether literal or figurative, the scope, the context, or parallel passages must decide the meaning.

V. In all tropical (figurative) language ascertain the point of resemblance, and judge the nature of the trope, and its kind, from the point of resemblance.

VI. In the interpretation of symbols, types, allegories, and parables, this rule is supreme. Ascertain the point to be illustrated; for comparison is never to be extended beyond that point—to all the attributes, qualities, or circumstances of the symbol, type, allegory, or parable.

VII. For the salutary and sanctifying intelligence of the oracles of God, the following rule is indispensable: We must come within the understanding distance. There is a distance, which is properly called the speaking distance, or the hearing distance, beyond which the voice reaches not, and the ear hears not. To hear another, we must come within that circle which the voice audibly fills. Now we may with propriety say, that as it respects God, there is an understanding distance. All beyond that distance cannot understand God; all within it can easily understand him in all matters of piety and morality.[5]

Campbell developed this approach decades before form criticism came into use in biblical study in America. And while the "understanding distance" step may have an element of mysticism in it, it seems appropriate to say that Campbell had a spirituality of reason rooted in the freedom of each person to explore, reflect on, and understand the scriptures. Reason was a gift of God to be used freely and faithfully.

Barton Warren Stone's spiritual sensitivity moved more to an emotional side than did Campbell's. While reason was very important for him, there were many occasions when his struggles over belief and vocation ran deep into his occasional feelings of lack of self-worth and the overpowering grace of God that gave his life meaning and form. Early in his ministry he became convinced that the Bible could be the primary source of authority on matters of faith and life.[6]

His ordination, in 1798 when he was twenty-six, was a potent example of that belief. "I went into the Presbytery, and when the question was posed, 'Do you receive and adopt the (Westminster) Confession of Faith, as containing the system of doctrine taught in the Bible?' I answered aloud, so that the whole congregation might hear, 'I do, as far as I see it consistent with the word of God.' No objection being made, I was ordained."[7]

In many ways the most important spiritual issue of the early Stone-Campbell Movement was the reality that theirs was a movement, not a static, unchanging entity like some of the denominations seemed to be in their times. For decades our tradition resisted the label "denomination," partly in the fear that it would identify us as just another frozen ecclesial body. It was believed that the use of that word would lessen the invitational character the founders sought to create, wherein any person seeking Christ as Savior could come here, without rules and requirements to be faced. It was a sincere belief that God's love would suffice to show us the way through the times and enable seeking people to choose us as the place where they could most fully experience faith without legalistic principles that required particular beliefs.

Our "Jubilee" Life

A biblical image that exemplifies this constant movement character is God's declaration that Israel should observe Jubilee in every fiftieth year. God had good reasons for insisting they do this. I suggest that the essence of "Movement," as it applies to the Stone-Campbell Movement, can be seen in the changes that happened to us over 200 plus years, viewed in five stages.

What is Jubilee? In Leviticus we learn that it was a time of rest and new beginning, a time to forgive debt, to remember and serve the poor.

Every forty-ninth year Yahweh requires the following
so that the household of freedom will not succumb
again to slavery: (1) Slaves are to be freed, (2) debts are
to be cancelled, (3) the land is to lie fallow, and (4) the
land (wealth or access to livelihood) is to be returned or
redistributed to its original holders. (Leviticus 25:23–24).
Even if the Jubilee year cannot be proved to have been
practiced, it has been remembered by Israel as what
Yahweh desires in the *oikos* (household) of freedom.[8]

Our son is a landscaper, and so he does a lot of planting. We
talked about annual and perennial flowers plants. He described
both, emphasizing perennials, plants that live all year and
year after year. In a real way Disciples are like a perennial plant
and these forty-nine-year periods between Jubilees, or Jubilee
seasons, are like stages in our life story as a movement. As we
examine these stages of the movement, it is important to note
attitudes towards race.

The First Jubilee season, the first half of the nineteenth
century, was frontier time. It was like the time when bulbs are
planted in fresh ground and begin breaking open to grow. Things
were messy. Growth was uneven. We were starting to walk and
we wanted our independence—even autonomy. We had few
clergy. We proclaimed a simple New Testament, Christ-centered
faith, with no suffocating rules and regulations. It was good news
to many people on the frontier, the rabble and the rich.

In those first years, however, the movement, like American
society at large, fell clearly into the camp of those who treated
race as an issue already in hand, with white persons the ones
for whom the land and its institutions, including churches,
were designed. To be sure, slaves could worship, either in the
balcony or outside, and, if they chose, in separate places. From
the beginning, though, separation was the racial norm.

The Second Jubilee, in the last half of the nineteenth century,
saw a more orderly expansion. Some vital "beginnings" flowered
as this perennial plant poked above the ground: in the Second

Jubilee many congregations were formed, a national convention, state associations for evangelism and Sunday school, mission societies, the educational formation of ministers and important cooperative work in church extension, benevolent care and pensions all had birth. We also got into some serious quarreling during this time, eventually leading to our separation into three streams of this flowing movement.

Much of this period was post-Civil War/Reconstruction, and the most specific response of Disciples was in the formation of schools in the South for children of former slaves. Under the leadership of the American Christian Missionary Society and Christian Women's Board of Mission, such institutions served for decades as a primary outreach effort of the white church. As well, this period saw the emergence of the Churches of Christ/Disciples of Christ, essentially a separate denomination of black Disciples in eastern Virginia and North Carolina, formed largely because of their refusal to be part of a church that relegated them to second-class status. In addition, at this point relations with American Indians were minimal at best.

The Third Jubilee, in the first half of the twentieth century, saw us going across the globe. We grew in spite of two major divisions in our tradition and flowered in some striking ways. The Disciples of Christ identity became clear in this time: an ecumenical partner/leader committed to justice and open education, with active global ministries and flourishing higher education institutions. Congregations gained strength, many now having full-time ministries. We weathered a harsh Depression and two painful world wars, and still grew. Some state associations had "missionary" efforts underway to form congregations for black persons as well as the continuing schools for their children.

Separation continued to be the guiding principle for whites and persons of color in the Movement. In *Plessy vs. Ferguson* (1896) the United States Supreme Court had made "separate but equal" (legal apartheid) the law of the land,[9] giving states and localities the freedom to establish separation (and inequality) in all facilities, and giving, as well, other institutions (such as the church) the informal license to continue the practice of separate racial systems. The Stone-Campbell Movement was no exception to this approach.

In 1917, forty-one black Disciples, gathering for an annual meeting in Nashville, Tennessee, formed the National Christian Missionary Convention. Under the leadership of Preston Taylor, a pastor and businessman, this body was formed to give a unique identity and community to black Disciples who found themselves no more than an object for mission by the white church. In at least one area, the tri-state region of Virginia, North Carolina, and South Carolina, an association of black Disciples formed with separate camps and, in time, a training program for ministers.

In 1913 Disciples began the Mexican Christian Institute (later named the Inman Mexican Center) in San Antonio, Texas, to provide educational and health services to Mexicans and Tejanos living in that area.

It was in this period also, in 1921, that Disciples began work among American Indians, with the formation of a mission effort in the Yakama Nation in Washington state.

Under the auspices of the United Christian Missionary Society, the All-Peoples Center in Los Angeles was formed in the 1940s to offer hospitality to "all peoples" in the crucible of World War II, and, over the years, as part of the Division of Homeland Ministries, it has come to be a most vital ministry serving the black community of that great city.

The Fourth Jubilee in the second half of the twentieth century brought restructure, both intentional and involuntary (the latter might be better called "destructure"). Many congregations, particularly those more than half a century old, went into decline, to be understood by some as a natural part of the life cycle,[10] leading to renewal if it was prayerfully sought. Mission policy changed from a traditional "we've come to bring the good news to you" way, to being partner-based with thriving churches across the world. Many of our people still don't understand that change.

With that change came the merger of the National Christian Missionary Convention (the legal name of the Convocation of black congregations) and the General Assembly of the Christian Church (Disciples of Christ) into one body. The National Convocation of the Christian Church (Disciples of Christ), serving primarily black Disciples of Christ congregations, continues as an important event in the alternate years to the General Assembly of the Christian Church (Disciples of Christ). The merger created several joint staff positions. The General Minister and President's office includes the Executive Secretary of the National Convocation, who is also an Associate General Minister and President. In the Division of Homeland Ministries four staff positions (evangelism, ministry, Christian education, women's ministries) have been jointly selected and administered. With some difficulties along the way, these shared positions have continued.

As this period evolved, two other movements became actively engaged. The North American Pacific/Asian Disciples community was formed as a vital presence in our life, holding a biennial conference, and a pastoral position in the Division of Homeland Ministries was developed to give oversight to this rapidly growing community and ministry. The Hispanic Disciples community has grown rapidly as well, with several regional "conventions" and a national Hispanic assembly every other year. The Central Pastoral Office for Hispanic Ministries emerged, with a pastoral leader for this vital community. It has become a critically important office for the Disciples church.

As our institutional life centralized and stabilized, anti-institutionalism was flourishing and society was becoming decentralized. It doesn't take a rocket scientist to figure out which force, restructure within or destructure without, had the most influence on the church's life and health. One brought some organizational consolidation, the other a major decline in many of the traditional forms that had been relied on to build and sustain the church.

Each of these times of Jubilee has seen a major transition to a fresh beginning for Disciples. In each of these, even though we haven't been very deserving or even aware of it, the one, grace-filled, and eternal God has offered new life to us. We have been moved to a different place.

This is the way God works with God's people—so far God has always given this people another opportunity to grow and bloom. As long as God gives us these times to start anew, which is what Jubilee is all about, we cannot be thankful enough. That each fifty years or so a new opportunity has come to the Disciples of Christ is a gift we dare not ignore. God loves us boldly.

And So We Stand at a New Beginning

We are beginning what I call our *Fifth Jubilee*. We are becoming more multiethnic, multiracial, multitheological, multinational, and multi-just about everything else than ever before. No longer are 90 percent of us to be found, as we often claimed in the past, within one hundred miles of a line from Pittsburgh to El Paso. Philadelphia, New York, Atlanta, Memphis, Orlando, Miami, the Dallas/Fort Worth metroplex, Los Angeles, and other places in the United States where our diversity and numbers are growing rapidly are far beyond that line The congregation with the largest number of participants is but a few years old and largely African American: New Directions in Memphis. That is a statement about the new congregation work happening in our lives.

We have had some recent storms. The failure of the National Benevolent Association and our stewardship struggles have hurt us and will do some real shaping of our character—for better we pray, not worse. Racism continues to plague us, and the very fact that many deny that it is still a real and evil force shows how real and evil it is. We still have miles to go before all of God's children in our midst will be received and fully accepted in this church.

We need the truthful dialogue that happens when people really love each other. We must, in this new Jubilee, learn to be lean, to travel light, to be accountable to each other, and to be collective in faith instead of just adoring of private religion. We must, in this new Jubilee, take seriously the call to become an anti-racist/pro-reconciling church. For those who think this is *passé,* then why is the incarceration rate of African American men in the U.S.A. four times greater than it was among black men in South Africa when apartheid was it its worst? This means either that African American men are among the worst criminals in history, or racism still rules in too much of America. Will we willingly seek to be transformed, beginning in the church, or will we deny the obvious facts? We can literally imitate the first call for Jubilee, as seen in Leviticus, where slaves are to be freed. For, as Douglas Meeks says, "Every forty-ninth year Yahweh requires...that the household of freedom will not succumb again to slavery."[11]

Many years ago I was giving a children's message in worship. I had some bean seeds. The text for the day was the mustard seed, but they're really tiny, so bean seeds were better. I held up these seeds. "What are these?" I asked the children. "Those are bean seeds," they said, with the clear implication that if I didn't know that, well I must have just fallen off the turnip truck. "Well, what do seeds do?" I asked. A little boy spoke up. "Seeds are tiny little trees, all folded up. When sunlight, water, and God all work on the cover, it breaks and the little tree unfolds and grows and stretches out to be as big as God means it to be." This seems like a rather perceptive description of the faith life to which Jesus calls us, a description that allows us to grow as a people beyond such sinfulness as institutionalized racism.

Questions for Reflection and Study

1. What factors led to the birth of the Disciples of Christ in frontier America?
2. What was the general attitude of early Disciples on matters related to race in American life?

3. Why are the Disciples of Christ called a "bridge" church?
4. In what ways might we be called a "white church"?
5. An "open church"?
6. A "changing church"?
7. What are at least three primary lessons to be learned from our history that can help us be a more inclusive church in the twenty-first century?
8. How do you describe a religious "movement"?
9. A "denomination"?
10. Which of these are the Disciples of Christ today and why?

CHAPTER 2

Born Apart

Chattel. The word means "Any moveable possession,"
Like a slave or a bondman that is not real estate.[1]

Slavery in the Western World

When the Stone-Campbell Movement was born in the
United States, "chattel" was the description that applied to
people of African ancestry, whose presence on this continent
and in the Sugar Islands of the Caribbean Sea had been made
possible by the massive slaving industry that had been going on
for nearly 300 years. That trade was one of the most profitable
in multi-national commercial history. It eventually brought,
by force, 15,000,000 African people to the West and Europe,
while over 9,000,000 perished at sea in what was called the
Middle Passage (the journey from Africa to America) of the
triangular route taken by most of the slaving ships, and whose
other two passages were from American to Europe and then
back to Africa.[2]

The reason for citing this is not to condemn or assign
guilt to our tradition or to that time of our birth, but simply

to acknowledge the reality that we were a product of an era with a violently enforced labor backbone that ultimately led us into a tragic Civil War. Agriculture and much of industry in the North American British colonies and then the United States were built, for centuries, on the backs of enslaved peoples. The racism that became a justifying rationale for slavery has now far outlived the very institution it was developed to support, and has become a long-lasting legacy of that cruel time.

As a result of inadequate education, which uses history written through rose-colored glasses (or written to protect white persons), most white Americans have not known the extent or duration of slavery in this land. These days "Americans seem perpetually startled at slavery," and it is, when addressed, treated as a "temporary aberration."[3] The reality is that slavery undergirded, indeed it drove, much of the agricultural and industrial development of this land. It also provided something of a model for other forms of servitude, such as child labor, that persisted during the early Industrial Revolution after the legal ending of slavery.

Disciples are certainly among those often surprised by the reality that the United States and some of our neighbors were indeed built on the backs of enslaved peoples.

This enslavement was not limited to Africans and their descendants. American Indians were used, primarily for gaining land, and in time Hispanic and Asian peoples were conscripted for their labor. In all cases of collective relations with communities of color, laws were made that reflected inequities that most white people accepted as part of their reality, some doing this as part of what they (the whites) believed was their due. People of color were less than humans, as if "white" was the true measure of humanness, and the further one was from "white," the less human that person was. Let's consider some examples of the parallels in time between the nurturing of this ideology of inferiority and the birth and growth of the Stone-Campbell Movement.[4]

Parallel Growths: A Religious Movement and an Ethical Aberration

In 1790, two years after Alexander Campbell's birth in Ireland, the young United States' Congress passed the first Naturalization Law. It stated that naturalization as a U.S. citizen was reserved for "any alien being a free white person." Had Thomas and Alexander Campbell been anything but free and white, they could not have become citizens of the United States.

In 1800, one year before Barton Stone went to the great revival in southern Kentucky and then hosted another at Cane Ridge, Thomas Jefferson had written, in a letter to Benjamin Rush, some of his most famous words: "I have sworn upon the altar of God eternal hostility against any form of tyranny over the mind of man." This came of his deep commitment to freedom of religion. Yet the same Thomas Jefferson had written, in his *Notes on the State of Virginia* some years earlier (1787), that African slaves were not the intellectual or emotional equals of white persons (Query XIV, Chapter 14),[5] and he owned 267 slaves (and freed only eight, five of whom were his blood kin) at his death in 1825.[6]

In 1828, just four years before the union of the Campbell and Stone movements, the Indian Removal Act was passed in the U.S. Congress. This resulted in the forced movement of tens of thousands of Cherokee and Creek Indians from southern states east of the Mississippi through Arkansas into what became Oklahoma Territory, their suffering leading to the name of the Trail of Tears. They were removed so white farmers could use their land. Though seldom mentioned in President Andrew Jackson's biographies, that Act was called, at the time, "the leading measure of the Jackson administration and the greatest matter that ever came before the Congress except for peace and war."[7]

By 1840, the year that Alexander Campbell founded Bethany College, 4.5 million people of European ancestry had crossed the Appalachian Mountains. In 1820, 120,000 Indians lived east of the Mississippi River, but by 1840 fewer than 30,000 were left. Their westward movement was not voluntary. In those same years the Stone-Campbell Movement flourished and grew, growth largely made up of those voluntarily migrating easterners turned westerners, and moving into land that had been occupied by native peoples.

In 1850, the year after the Stone-Campbell Movement held its first national convention in Cincinnati, the U.S. Congress enacted the Fugitive Slave Act. This was a concession to the southern states in return for the admission of Mexican territories, particularly California, into the Union as nonslave states. The Fugitive Slave Act made it easy for slave owners to recapture ex-slaves or simply to pick up blacks they claimed had run away.[8]

In 1857, between the years when James Turner Barclay served in Palestine as the Stone-Campbell Movement's first missionary (two terms, 1851–54, 1858–62),[9] the United States Supreme Court rendered the Dred Scott ruling, in which Chief Justice Taney wrote that the slave Dred Scott could not sue for his freedom because he was not a person, but property.[10]

We could add many more examples in history, but the purpose here is not just to study history. Rather it is to reinforce that the development of the Stone-Campbell Movement was historically parallel to events that happened in support of the separation of races in the United States. As a result, much of who our church was and has become is a product of that culture of separation.

The History of Race

We turn now to the history of race in the United States and then the reactions of people of our movement to this culture of separation.

The idea of race did not originate in North America, but it is young, as far as the human story goes. Before European exploration began in the fifteenth century, race had not been a named issue in the human experience. Certainly people with differing skin colors had been around each other. But no evidence shows that those differences were deemed as having anything to do with variances in ability or humanness. As Europeans explored the world, buttressed by papal bulls and royal commissions (like Ferdinand and Isabella's commission to Christopher Columbus) it became important to them to see themselves as superior to those they found in the new lands.

In spite of the Moors from Africa bringing to Europe much of the knowledge that powered the Renaissance, this need for superiority made it more acceptable to possess the lands they "discovered." The doctrine of "discovery," a unique creation of European expansionism, was their guiding force, and this allowed them to "discover" and claim any lands in the name of their land and the faith, no matter who had lived in and, quite obviously, "discovered" that land before.[11] As a result, they found a way to name those who occupied those lands as inferior to the European "discoverers," and to make raw might and deception the arbiters of who won the day.

Thus, when the first ship to deliver Africans to North American soil put in at Jamestown in 1619, race was brought to the new continent's mainland. Ironically, the ship that carried those nineteen indentured servants was named the *Jesus,* a Dutch vessel engaged in transporting humans for service, part of that common international commerce of the day.

Those first Africans in Virginia were not slaves in the same way that people later understood the term. They were indentured; that is, they could work for some years and thus gained their freedom. But many whites were also indentured, and because of shared rebellions of white and black servants, the authorities of Virginia soon determined that blacks and whites were to be in servitude of different kinds. Whites were indentured with the possibility of freedom. Blacks were declared to be *chattel,* property, and freedom could not come to them unless granted by an owner.[12]

How was this distinction made possible? Race was already becoming a believed fact in Europe. It was rather simple to determine a difference between servants of European origin and slaves of African heritage. Inferiority was already attributed to the African people. This was, as well, a condition attributed to American Indians. They were not European, not white, and therefore inferior to whites and deserving of treatment appropriate to their standing, low as it was.

Slavery had existed in much of history, but never before, to our knowledge, had people of one skin color enslaved those of another color. At this particular point in time (the fifteenth-sixteenth centuries C.E.), "Whites viewed the enslavement of whites as illegitimate, while the enslavement of Africans was acceptable."[13]

Race, and the collective use of power to enforce the prejudice that race consciousness created, became a fact: *racism*. Racism was born in the crucible of European expansion. At its root, economics drove what became one of the great moral crimes of history.

Racism persisted and grew to the point where its judgments became larger than the slavery it had unleashed. The Lincoln-Douglas debates for the United States Senate in Illinois in 1858 remain one of the most famous features of any political contest in the United States. They pitted a leader of the powerful Democratic Party (founded over fifty years earlier by Thomas Jefferson), Stephen Douglas, against an emerging leader of the new Republican Party, Abraham Lincoln. The issue of race was a major theme of that struggle. On July 9, 1858, Stephen Douglas stated his position on these matters quite clearly:

> In my opinion this government of ours is founded on the white basis. It was made by the white man, for the benefit of the white man, to be administered by white men... I am opposed to taking any step that recognizes the Negro man or the Indian as the equal of the white man. I am opposed to giving him a Voice in the administration of the government. I would extend

to the Negro, and the Indian, and to all dependent races every right, every privilege, and every immunity consistent with the safety and welfare of the white races; but equality they never should have, either political or social, or in any other respect whatever. My friends, you see that the issues are distinctly drawn.[14]

Stephen Douglas won that Senate election in 1858.

Following the Civil War, while slavery had legally ended, racism became stronger and new forms of servitude were rapidly created. The power of racism was showing itself as even stronger and more violent than the slavery it had supported. Like a child who becomes larger, noisier, and more powerful than its parent, racism persisted and grew in America. Reconstruction was short-lived, the land of American Indian nations was taken from them as treaties were abrogated and, finally, the Dawes Act, passed in 1887, made possible the eventual taking of some 90,000,000 acres of tribal lands. This became homesteading land for westward moving white persons. Many Disciples of Christ churches were established on lands that had been tribal possessions.

The *Plessy vs. Ferguson* (1896) decision of the United States' Supreme Court, established the principle of "separate but equal" facilities as the law of the land. Based on a Louisiana case where a black man sought to ride without separation from whites in a railroad car, the state held that the railroad could determine where white persons and persons of color could ride on the train. The state won the case and this gave legalized authorization to states and localities to form "separate but equal" schools, restaurants, hotels, neighborhoods, even public rest rooms and water fountains. Called the "Jim Crow laws" the vast majority of the time these laws allowed "separate and *un*equal" accommodations. The federal government took no hand in righting this wrong. It lasted until 1954 when the *Brown vs. Board of Education* decision of the Supreme Court nullified this doctrine. It took some years for this to become reality—in fact, separation or apartness (known in South Africa as "apartheid") still persists in some informal ways and hidden places.

The Stone-Campbell Movement's Responses

How did people in the Stone-Campbell Movement respond to this fact of their life? We need here to remember that the Stone-Campbell Movement was more a product of the American frontier than a shaper of it. The new political and economic freedom, a passion to overcome divisions, a felt need to give voice to one's own faith and not just repeat the creedal formulae of others, a desire for a simple way to worship and serve—all gave birth to the fresh movement in this young land. Social issues were secondary for most of the people in this new movement. For most of them society's treatment of social matters was adequate, and these were not considered to be particularly germane religious concerns.

The *Encyclopedia of the Stone-Campbell Movement* gives a bluntly honest picture of attitudes in the young movement:

> The story of race relations in the Stone-Campbell Movement begins largely with the attitudes toward slavery held by early leaders and members. The full spectrum of ante-bellum positions was represented in the churches of the Movement, from Alexander Campbell's Jeffersonian opposition to slavery, to James Shannon's fire-eating advocacy of it, to Barton W. Stone's endorsement of immediate abolition. Belief in the superiority of the white race, however, was an almost universal assumption across the board.[15]

From the beginning separation was the norm, with Cane Ridge Church having a balcony where slaves sat, and quite soon separate churches being formed for and by slaves and freed persons of color. While the Movement never excluded person of color from participation, this separation persisted and still does in many places.

Even Barton Stone, whose support of abolition has been noted, was an advocate, for a time, of resettlement of freed slaves to Africa. While Alexander Campbell opposed slavery, he characterized the problem with it as primarily social, not political or moral.[16]

After the Civil War, former slaves who had been worshiping in mixed race congregations formed their own churches, not wanting the "separateness" that still prevailed. Missionary efforts were organized for freed peoples, efforts all under white control that were sometimes resented and even resisted. Finally, as stated before, Preston Taylor of Nashville, Tennessee, who had been born a slave and became a lay preacher and active businessman, led in organizing the National Christian Missionary Convention, a gathering of black Disciples of Christ congregations. This was formed in 1917 in part to combat racial injustices that were being experienced by African Americans. A fair level of cooperation emerged, but always within the polite norms of church and society. Cooperation happened within the International Convention of Christian Churches (Disciples) and under restructure a merger was developed, but with black Disciples still holding to their identity through the National Convocation of the Christian Church (Disciples of Christ).[17]

The work of three Disciples of Christ leaders of the nineteenth century bear brief examination and they reflect who we were and are on this great issue. Alexander Campbell was a delegate to the Virginia Constitutional Convention in 1829. He went with the hope that the new constitution would include a provision for the elimination of slavery by establishing a set date after which all persons born slaves would become free.[18] Campbell was confronted with some political heavyweights in that Convention: James Madison, James Monroe, John Marshall, and others, all supporters of slavery, and was unable to pursue that interest to a successful conclusion.

His approach has been called a "calculated emancipation," and it was shared by a number of other early leaders of the church, such as Walter Scott. He spoke of being "no friend to slavery," yet unable to speak out because it "would be folly." When we look at the numbers we can understand Scott's caution. With a total population of 12.8 million in the U.S., more than 2 million were slaves.[19] Advocates of slavery believed that any flagging of control would mean economic and social chaos.

The second person we examine is James Shannon, who was a college president and an outspoken advocate of slavery. He presided at Bacon College in Kentucky, then, in succession, at the University of Missouri and Culver-Stockton College. He found the New Testament to be supportive of slavery, saying that neither Jesus nor the apostles interfered with it, and indeed they counseled slaves to be "obedient to their masters."

The final personal examination is of James A. Garfield, who served as president of Hiram College, as a Union Army officer, and was later elected President of the United States. Garfield was an abolitionist, and though on good terms with other leaders of the Movement, including advocates of the aforementioned "calculated emancipation," it is a fair question to ask whether, had Garfield been able to serve his term as President (he was assassinated shortly after election) would the nation as well as the Movement have moved far more quickly to right the wrongs that collective racism was inflicting?

It is accurate, then, to surmise that the spirit of the Stone-Campbell Movement continued, and to some extent still continues, to reflect that broad spectrum of responses to racism, from a kind of benign acceptance of the *status quo*; through a calculated and deliberate approach to change, to overt efforts to do away with the injustices that racism perpetrates on people of color that enable white persons to have more power and privilege. As we shall see later, though, the eradication of institutional racism would mean *all* would have power and privilege. White power and privilege would be changed only to the extent that we have it in unequal amounts compared to persons of color.

Where does this leave us today? What do we need to do? We have choices. We can do nothing and hope it all works its way out. Or we can act, acknowledging that the first place to begin acting is within ourselves. If we grew up during this time, then we, like other institutions of our time, have lingering, often strong, evidences of racism. What are these evidences and how can we deal with them? We turn to these concerns as this exploration continues.

Some Questions for Reflection and Study

1. What are some ways in which our church's history reflected its culture? Does this still happen?
2. Are Disciples still "startled" by the continuing presence of racism? How do we show this?
3. What can we learn from the "parallel" histories of the Disciples of Christ and racial separation in the United States?
4. Do we still reflect the "broad spectrum" described by the nineteenth-century beliefs of Alexander Campbell, James Shannon, and James A. Garfield? If so, how would you summarize those beliefs, and what forms do they take today?
5. Where on that spectrum can your congregation as a whole be found?
6. What do you believe Jesus would say to Disciples about racism today?

CHAPTER 3

Covenantal Values

An Overview

The church, the "body of Christ" (1 Cor. 12:27), is a social system. It is people, brought together, who when together, are an entity different from the sum of the parts. This is what theologian Letty Russell calls "the gift of synergy" (the total effect is greater than the sum of the parts).[1]

Human and Social Systems

It was a special moment for us to see each of our grandsons the first time and then from there on. Here were these round mounds of sound, flesh, eyes, hair, nose, noise, and snuggling. Those little organisms grow, suck food, cry, smile, gurgle, coo, kick, and play in a combination of interworking parts, none of which could survive alone. Together, though, these interact and have become more than fine little human beings. They are what some experts call "biological systems." Whenever different parts work together and become something more than they are either alone or added up, they can be called a system.

The church, whether in a congregation, cluster, denomination, or ecumenical grouping, is a combination of parts.

The congregation brings individuals together. The middle judicatory brings congregations (and individuals) together. The denomination brings judicatories (and individuals and congregations) together. The grouping brings denominations together. In every expression, it is a "system," in which varying parts come together and become something other than the sum of these parts.

So here we are, with physical organisms like our grandsons, and social organisms like our congregations. These organisms differ in many ways. Waylon and Johnny (those little fellows' names) sweat, eat, fuss, mess, grin (do they ever!), and generally charm anyone who is near. Our congregation worships, serves, prays, recruits, sings, greets, supports, and generally loves anyone who is near.

They sound quite similar in a way, don't they?

Certainly they are, yet they aren't. The little boys are biological/emotional/intellectual organisms and the church is a social organism. They are each, though, organisms and they are each "systems." This means that each brings together various elements into relationship, and, together, these elements form the "whole" that is the little boys in the case of Waylon and Johnny, and in the other case is the congregation.

In Waylon and Johnny those elements include digestion, neurology, muscles, skeletal structure, urinary, genital, mental, emotional, and above all, spiritual processes.

In the church those elements include leadership, communication, organizational structure, normative behavior, spiritual beliefs, and collective values, to name just some core elements.

In each, the elements, added together, become the whole.

Just as Johnny is not identical to Waylon, so the congregation my spouse and I belong to (Bethany Beach Christian Church) is not exactly like yours.

No two individuals are exactly alike, nor are two social systems, such as congregations. But each has certain core elements.

Let's translate this to a denomination: the Christian Church (Disciples of Christ). *Who* are we? Like individual and social organisms, we have a particular identity and life as a whole denomination.

We were born on the American frontier, led by religious pioneers who believed that what was most important was to simply restore the New Testament church in every way possible. They were part of a movement that emphasized freedom, individualism, and a rejection of any kinds of authority that sought to form and constrain the beliefs of others.

After all, the frontier was not made up of the rich, elite, and powerful of the nation, or those who had gotten status from heritage or money. It was a raw place, a demanding, inspiring, sometimes messy context in which men and women and families survived often only by being obstinate, strong, and faithful. Many of them chose it because there they could live as they chose.

My great, great-grandfather, Thomas Hobgood, led his family from eastern Carolina to western Kentucky sometime before 1839 so he could farm where and as he wanted, with no one breathing down his neck. He was typical. Of such were the Christians and Disciples made. If they were going to conform, it would be to a norm of self-sufficiency and independence, not one of subservience and dependence.

It's important to note that few of those early Disciples had slave holdings. Most of them couldn't afford any. This, however, didn't keep them from falling into the mentality of the times, which said that people who were not white were not fully human.

This movement, made up of some called Christians and others known as Disciples, very soon took on a character and identity of its own, seen in some those core elements.

The Importance of Values

One of the core elements of any social system is its values. Values are as vital to a social system as circulation is to a biological one. In the mid-1960s a *process of valuing* became part of the language and discipline of many who sought to develop human potential. Louis E. Raths, Merrill Harmin, and Sidney B. Simon published *Values and Teaching* and it quickly moved to the center of much that was offered in enabling people to better know themselves and their ways of living.[2]

Defining values as "those elements that show how a person has decided to use his/her life,"[3] these teachers proceeded to identify seven criteria that must be part of the process of valuing. For a value to result, all of the seven must apply:

1. *Choosing freely.* If something is to guide one's life, it must be chosen. There can be no coercion if this is to be a behavior that has value to the person.
2. *Choosing from among alternatives.* Only when a choice has been made is it a value. For example, eating is not a value, for we've no choice if we are to stay alive. Liking French cuisine can be a value, though, because there are choices of food preferences.
3. *Choosing after thoughtful consideration of the consequences.* A choice calls for reflecting on potential results. Blind choice is not a choice.
4. *Prizing and cherishing.* A chosen behavior is like a beloved possession. If we value it we will cherish, prize, and protect it.
5. *Affirming.* A consciously chosen value will be affirmed to others. We will be willing to speak for it, willingly claiming it to any who will hear.
6. *Acting upon choices.* A value is not inert and lifeless. When we choose it we will do it, else it is not a value, just an idea. We will also move to support our actions—for example, we may associate with others who have a similar value.
7. *Repeating.* A value is not a one-time happening. It will show up in many places in our lives. It will guide us to places. It will frame actions.[4]

Values are sometimes confused with "norms." Norms are standards or rules of behavior for a group, which, though followed, may or may not be chosen by individual members.

To comfortably maintain one's membership in the group persons will follow the group's norms. I remember asking a woman named Eleanor why no one sat in the first three pews in the sanctuary. "I don't know why others don't do it, but I don't sit there because sitting in the front gives me a crick in my next. The pulpit is so high that it's a strain to watch you preach." For her, it was a chosen behavior, a value based on the desire not to have pain in the neck. For some who'd never sat in the front, though, avoiding the front pews and sitting further back was not a choice, simply a behavior done because, they said, "No one else sits up there." Normative behavior is the way groups move, either by collective decision, example, or rote, to shape the ways people act in the group. They are not prized or even actions to be affirmed. While they are a core element, and some of these are necessary for a group's life, they are often followed without even thinking about them. They simply happen.

I recall an important college conversation with a fellow student named Fred, who was two years ahead of me. I had developed a lot of respect for Fred, but it was hard to say why. Up to that time I had been living in large part just as I'd been taught—without thinking, just copying. Examples had been set and I had followed. Beyond that, I did what I most enjoyed or what was necessary. One day Fred observed that doing a certain thing was "against my principles." For the first time I began to contemplate what it means to have "principles," or chosen guidelines that set boundaries on what one does. In later years I came to see these as ethically based values.

Core Values

In recent years a refinement of values theory has led to a particular kind of values called "core values." While the originators of values clarification didn't speak of core values, their work leads naturally to the conclusion that some values will define the very character of a person. Without a "core value" a person would not be the same.

Exercise is of high value to me. If possible, I exercise at least five days a week, for up to ninety minutes. It makes me healthier, more productive, and I feel better. Like eating fish, it is a choice I make and follow regularly. I could, though, be myself without it. On the other hand, having family times together is so important that without such times I would not be who I am. Every year our family has at least two reunions of four days to a week. We anticipate these with passion. Here we can see exercise as a value, family time as a core value.

A friend of mine loves movies. He sees many new releases and if there are no new ones nearby, he will see a show he has seen before. He often travels, and many evenings, after work and dinner are through, he goes to movies. He also reads voraciously. Much of his reading is for professional purposes, but he reads good literature, from classics to contemporary novels. Much of his thinking and belief system is shaped by what he learns from his reading. For him movies are something he values, but his reading defines his very being—it is a core value.

The Church and Values

Any community of people with a common cause gathers around shared beliefs and values. Some of these are implanted at the beginning; others have been incorporated during that community's lifetime. All are subject to some change, but there is an enduring character to these commonly chosen and practiced values that enables them to define that particular community. They are living guides, not dead traditions.

If a community is a living social being, then can it not have chosen values, just as a living human being can? I believe it can, and it can have core values. I have chosen to name five core values, which I believe do more to define the Disciples of Christ than most other aspects of our community life. Some time ago a colleague called them "covenantal values," and this name has held. The name is rooted in the belief that these are values that have not only defined us, but have been fundamental to God's "covenant of love that binds us to God and one another."[5] A summary of these covenantal values follows. Each will be discussed in deeper detail in separate chapters.

The Confession of Faith in Jesus Christ as Lord and Savior

"I believe that Jesus is the Christ, the Son of the Living God, and I accept him as my Lord and Savior."

This is a deeply spiritual confession and experience that calls for repentance as a step in meaningful confession. The confession has its biblical base in Matthew 16:16, Peter's declaration: "You are the Messiah, the Son of the living God." From our earliest times, we Disciples have held this to be our only "test of fellowship," or requirement for membership. People make this confession at baptism and at the reaffirmation of faith, and increasingly, as we move from congregation to congregation, we are asked to re-announce our faith through the confession.

When our founders made this confession, they meant more than a sweet and rather gentle announcement. Their confession was not a tame, lame one. It was of substance. It took its power from a crucified Savior. Jesus died to show us the depth of God's love for us. He suffered with and for us. We were, and are, worth his death. Only after death does resurrection come.

Ours is not a triumphalist faith as much as a suffering one. We do not proclaim "victory" as much as we do "sacrificial love." We "serve a Risen Savior,"[6] as the hymn "He Lives" declares, but first we worship a "crucified God," said theologian Jurgen Moltmann.[7] It is in Jesus' death, not just in his resurrection, that we are shown the power of God's love.

"I believe that Jesus is the Christ, Son of the Living God, and I accept him as my Lord and Savior."

I urge people to recite the confession daily in prayers, and to meditate on the currently popular question, "What would Jesus do?" The answer is clear. It is *not* what Jesus *would* do, but what he has *already done*: he has suffered for and with us.

The Open and Inclusive Lord's Supper

Again we are reaching deep into our roots as a movement. In events in the church in which they had earlier affiliation, Thomas and Alexander Campbell both experienced a "fenced" table. That is, the practice of humans barring others from the Lord's Supper. Barton Stone felt even more strongly that the Lord's Supper should be open to all Christians. Consequently, in some parts of our tradition we have always practiced an open communion and all began to do this after the first few decades. We believe that no one has the right to bar anyone else from partaking of the "body and blood" of Jesus Christ in the eucharistic meal.

God is the host at this table, not us. We may set it, but God in Jesus invites all to "examine [them]selves, and only then eat of the bread and drink of the cup" (1 Cor. 11:28).

This is, from our standpoint, a call to radical hospitality. One of the rules of Torah, or the commandments of Hebrew scripture, is *hospitality*.[8] In this biblical hospitality, the host is honored when a guest comes to the home. The home becomes the guest's home. Indeed, there are no guests in this hospitable house.

This kind of inclusiveness is the way we are called to shape the whole life of the church. The Lord's table is not only a particular worship act, but it is a model for everything we do in the church. It forms and informs our whole life. What good is it, for example, for a congregation to say, "All are welcome at the table," and then not be willing to include some into membership in the congregation? What if "Joe" can partake of the Great Meal, but cannot qualify for membership because he was not baptized properly?

A serious approach to the Lord's Supper will lead us to take a serious look at everything we do as congregations. To be faithful as Disciples of Christ we need to be consistent.

The Ministry of All Believers

This value is rooted in the biblical truth that God places spiritual gifts in all who believe, and places a call to ministry upon everyone.

Our founders practiced the Reformation concept of "the priesthood of all believers." Reformers had lifted this in contrast to the appalling corruption they found in the priesthood in the church of their time. This shared ministry was, they believed, God's will. All Christians can be priests to one another. Stone-Campbell leaders agreed. They found much of the religious leadership of their time to appear arrogant, insisting that people believe as they dictated.

In resisting this concentration of spiritual authority, the founders became somewhat anti-clerical. Stone and the Campbells didn't object to ordained clergy, but they did not hold this as primary among the necessary elements of the church. In fact, Disciples had relatively few clergy in our first fifty years. Lay elders often led congregations. When we did begin setting some apart for pastoral roles, they did not supplant elders in authority.

In the twenty-first century we have come to believe that all persons are ordained to ministry at their baptisms. All persons, Paul says, are "given the manifestation of the Spirit for the common good" (1 Cor. 12:7).

One church prints, on their Sunday bulletin, "University Christian Church. Staff: 3 pastors and 300 ministers." In this church, says one pastor friend of mine, there are no volunteers, only disciples. This means we are under discipline to follow Jesus. This leaves us no wiggle room, no way out of service. There is a call on each and every one of us to be ministers (servants) of, for, and with Jesus Christ.

The Love of Unity, Wherein We Are Called to Lead in the Healing of the Broken Church and World

In his last prayer, according to John, Jesus prayed, "that they [his present and future disciples] may all be one" (Jn. 17:21). Barton Stone said, "For 32 years of my ministry I have kept in view the unity of Christians as my polar star."[9] Stone often used this metaphor, "polar star," to describe the importance of Christian unity in his understanding of ecclesiology.

Thomas Campbell, in 1809, wrote in his *Declaration and Address,* "The church of Christ on earth is essentially, intentionally and constitutionally one." Stone and the Campbells believed that human opinion had divided the church, though it had begun as one. They were convinced that if those human opinions could be cut through, God's given unity would emerge as intended.

Jesus Christ, and the frontier reformers, were speaking of a unity that already exists, that God has already created. So it becomes our task, not to unite Christ's body, but to recognize the fact that God has already created unity. It is not our responsibility to create unity, but to live into God's unity. Ours is not to presume the power to create, but to humbly receive what God creates.

The word *ecumenical* comes from the Greek *"oikumene,"* which means "the whole created order." It was used in the Bible to describe the *"oikos,"* the household of God, which is all of creation.

We are called to live into the already united creation, to recognize the wonder of God's creation. We are to build, not tear down. We are to heal and not wound. We are to celebrate unity, not cause disunity.

This is a unique vocation of Disciples. Because we began out of the disunity of the early American church, we have long been on the forefront of unity efforts among churches. In the twenty-first century we are called to be in the vanguard of unity efforts not only in the church, but in all the created order.

Restoring the Justice of God: A Radical Commitment to the Truth That God's Whole Creation Is Good

In God's realm all stand on level ground:

Every valley shall be lifted up,
    and every mountain and hill be made low;

the uneven ground shall become level,
and the rough places a plain.
Then the glory of the LORD shall be revealed.

(Isa. 40:4–5a)

What this says to us is that all creation is equally loved and valued. We dare not discard anyone or anything made by God. If we believe that God is ruler, sovereign of the universe, then it follows that everything God has created, all humans and all else, is of royal blood. To follow the metaphor, we are all princesses and princes. Every plant, tree, rock, and grain of sand is part of the royal garden.

How is royalty treated? In royal traditions, royalty is given special treatment. In this realm, where every thing and being is royal, special treatment is due. Walter Brueggemann said that God is "a resilient and relentless advocate of and agent for justice, which entails the complete reordering of power arrangements in the earth."[10]

The justice of God calls us to give back to all people and creation the esteem and treatment due that which is "of God."

All evangelism, mission, and stewardship take root in this belief. Justice tells us how to live our individual lives, and it tells the church how to live its collective life.

Why is this of particular importance to Disciples? Are not all people of faith called to practice God's justice? In reply, we might paraphrase Barton Stone's rationale for the use of the title "Christian" when he said, "We are not the only Christians, but we are Christians only." Here we can say, "We are not the only just ones, but we are to practice justice in all we do."

What makes the practice of justice so important for Disciples? We need to understand that we are the outgrowth of God's radical justice. We were formed as a wholly egalitarian church. We had no hierarchy; no one was more or less important than anyone else. Using the image that the prophet Isaiah gives us (Isa. 40:4–5a), all stood on level ground. Only a wholly just God could call us into this way of understanding creation.

The justice of God must form our practice of life; justice should shape everything we do. For the Disciples of Christ, new church formation and the anti-racism initiative are grounded in the justice of God. Youth ministries and the transformation of existing congregations are part of the practice of the justice of God. Forming and reforming leaders and witnessing to God's sacrificial love across the globe all grow from our passion to be part of the justice of God. Evangelism, in which we have not been very proactive in recent decades, requires passion because only an evangelizing church can truly witness to God's just love for all.

Covenantal Values and Disciples Identity

Just as an individual has a name and an identity, so does a social organism. It is an amazing part of our story that even in the rather undisciplined time of the American frontier, the Christians/Disciples were being formed with particular values. These did not always come easily. All parties did not always agree on the relative worth of these values, but all parties knew that some form of identity would be essential.

For many decades we resisted the use of the word *denomination* to categorize ourselves. Calling ourselves a "Movement" or a "Brotherhood," we continued to claim a nondenominational identity. The assumption was that to be named a denomination would make us just like all the others. One definition of the word *denomination* is "name." The very name of the church of which the Campbells had been members, Old-Light Anti-Burgher Seceder Presbyterians, suggests several schisms. The founders did not want to be seen as another schismatic group. One of the difficult processes of the Disciples early life was, then, how to have an identity without simply being just another self-created/perpetuating church with a name to denote us from others.

These qualities, which we are calling core values, became some of our defining marks. They are values because they are more than only intellectually held beliefs; they are descriptive of the way we are and act as a people. They are cherished and repeated practices. We witness to them. Certainly a characteristic of Disciples is that not all of us will agree on the five that I have identified, and that's fine, because we'd become too compartmentalized if this were the case. We'd lose a degree of our *naiveté* and frontier-rooted independence if we were to be all of one accord. In fact, some would argue that this very independence is a core value for us. Whether it is an essential value is an open question. Rather than get trapped in this argument, however, I choose to leave this open. To do so is more in keeping with our temperament.

The Intent to Dismantle Racism in the Christian Church (Disciples Of Christ)

Even as this is being written, the office of Reconciliation Mission is in a period of evaluation and transition. Insufficient funds have been a continuing issue.

This ministry of the Christian Church (Disciples of Christ) began in the late 1960s for the purpose of developing reconciliation between economic and racial/ethnic communities in North America. The civil rights movement was a very active and sometimes abrasive part of American life. A short time earlier, black activists had demanded reparations from the largely white churches who, they said, had been very much a part of racism in the U.S.A., if not by overt intention, then certainly by their deafeningly loud silence.

While a more detailed history of this part of modern Disciples history must be found elsewhere, the focus here is on the relationship of contemporary anti-racism efforts to the five Disciples covenantal values described briefly in this chapter.

Each of these values grows out of the impulse of God's consuming love for all of creation. Our belief in Jesus Christ as Savior of all, our practice of sacramental and active inclusiveness, the commitment we hold to shared servant ministry, our passion for unity, and our deep trust in God's justice all speak of a people who are openly pursuing a world where racism, like other forms of senseless injustice, is no more. In point of fact, each of these values contains the seeds of the truth that God's family cannot be separated into parts as racism has, too often, done.

I will take the position that these core values cannot be defined as constructs that have been developed by humans to justify our often-destructive actions. I contend, though, that racism *is* such a construct, and that, just as humans have done theological injustice by imposing their views on others, so also in allowing racism to become a dogma that shapes our culture have we let human opinions replace God's passionate desire.

Seen in this light, the dismantling of racism is a deep spiritual necessity. My reason for engaging this theme is to say that the dismantling of racism can be natural to Disciples—because of who we have been, are, and will be—as is each of the covenantal values. More than just being one more program, and beyond the good intentions and works of well-meaning Disciples, *anti-racism must become part of our very culture as a people of faith.* It should become a sixth core value. Though, unlike the others, it has not been consciously held to from the beginning, it is a necessary value for this new century.

Some Questions for Reflection and Study

1. How can you define a value? A norm?
2. What is the difference between a value and a core value?
3. What are *your* core values?
4. What do you believe are the core values of your congregation?
5. Do you believe that combating racism should be a core value of the Disciples?
6. If so, how would you do work to make it so? If not, why not?

CHAPTER 4

I Confess That Jesus Is the Christ

It was the morning of my eleventh birthday, and we were standing amid 300 to 400 people on the banks of the Momboyo River at Lotumbe, the Congo. My father took my hand and asked, "Chris, do you believe that Jesus is the Christ, the Son of the Living God?" I responded, "I believe that Jesus is the Christ, Son of the Living God, and accept him as Lord and Savior," and was baptized.

It was Sunday, January 1, 2006. My spouse Cary Meade and I stood with Sir Walter Scott, our pastor at Bethany Beach Christian Church, and he asked, "Do you believe that Jesus is the Christ?" We said, "We believe that Jesus is the Christ, Son of the Living God, and accept him as Lord and Savior," and were welcomed into that congregation.

A few things had happened between those two days. Cary Meade has lived an exemplary life as teacher, friend, parent, and a quietly powerful person. I've had several positions in ministry as well as a life as a father and partner and brief careers in football and music.

But because we are Disciples of Christ, no matter how long we've lived, where we've been, or what positions we've held, this confession of faith remains our sole test of fellowship, and *every* Disciple is asked to submit to this test sincerely and publicly.

I cannot say that I've fully understood it each time I've said it. (By the way, this is now something I confess daily in prayers, and I commend this practice to all who claim Jesus Christ as Savior.) In addition, I do not claim to believe at this moment that each time I say it in the future it will be with anything near to full understanding of its meaning, either.

What we *can* say, though, is that every time we make this confession we are reaching to grow in faith and understanding. The moment growth stops, then spiritual death sets in. Poet Robert Browning said, a long time ago, "[One's] reach must exceed [one's] grasp, or what's a heaven for?"[1] We can and sometimes do reach further and further, never being complete in faith and life.

From Our Birth as Disciples

From our birth as a people, Disciples/Christians have said that the confession of faith in Jesus Christ is our one test of fellowship and faith. Some may say, "Well, that's not much to pin a theology on!" And we say, "What more is needed?" We focus on this because, as Robert Cornwall, a pastor and historian of our heritage states it, "The Stone-Campbell Movement has, from the beginning, sought to base its theology on scripture, and has been averse to making post biblical creedal statements normative tests of fellowship."[2] "Post biblical creedal statements" means anything councils such as those in Nicea and other places came up with to give words to what people believed or were expected to believe.

The confession is biblical, to be found in Matthew 16:16, Mark 8:29, and Luke 9:20. This is critical to its becoming our sole test of fellowship.

We've said that if a "value" is a belief that you hold and practice repeatedly and are willing to proclaim to others, then a core value is a value that defines who you are.

For us, it is a *core value* to proclaim Jesus Christ as Savior and to make that the *only* faith test people must meet to be a part of this faith community.

Our story points to this confession as one of the most important *core values* of the Christian/Disciples heritage.

Alexander Campbell and Barton Stone, the most prominent early leaders of the two movements that joined to form us, didn't necessarily agree on their christology (that is, the study of *who* Jesus Chris was and is). Campbell believed Jesus was the full incarnation—or enfleshment—of God; fully divine, he was atoning, sacrificing, and kingly. Stone held that Jesus Christ was subordinate to God, but was the mediator between God and humans, and revealed to humans God's full image.[3] To both, however, the confession of faith was essential.

Your christology and mine may differ. We don't and won't always agree, and that gladdens the hearts but sometimes maddens the spirits of Disciples. "If they would only agree with *me!*" some people of faith say. Not so with Disciples. Yet for all our subtle and big differences, the confession of faith in Jesus Christ as God's Son and our Lord and Savior stands less because of any uniform, identical cookie-cutter belief about Jesus Christ, and more because of its spiritual impact.

To really confess is to enter a deeply spiritual experience that calls for repentance, renouncing our alienation from God and indifference to the rest of God's creation. With this confession we declare ourselves no longer our own rulers.

When our founders made the confession it was more than a gentle announcement. One of their best descriptions of the confession and its theological content is made in Walter Scott's "Five Finger Exercise." This exercise is a summary of the plan of salvation, which Scott, for a time the primary evangelist in the Campbell part of the Stone-Campbell "stream," used in his preaching:

- *First finger: confession of faith.* "Faith [is] belief in God's offer of salvation through Jesus Christ, [and it was] the first step in the experience of conversion and regeneration."[4]

- *Second finger: repentance of sins.* This is a genuine acknowledgement of our brokenness.
- *Third finger: baptism.* Here the believer obeys the Christ whose love for that believer came first. Here God meets us in the cleansing waters and provides assurance that our sins are remitted.
- *Fourth finger: forgiveness of sins.* God continues to act by giving forgiveness to the believer.
- *Fifth finger: gift of the Holy Spirit.* This is God's continuing gift. Scott often added eternal life, almost like a sixth finger.[5]

It is clear that theirs was not a tame, lame confession. It was of substance. It took its power from a crucified Savior. Jesus died to show us the depth of God's love for us. He suffered with and for us. We were, and are, worth his death. Only after death does resurrection come.

This confession produces both individual change and community covenant. Covenant is critical to life as a church. "The Preamble to the Design of the Christian Church (Disciples of Christ)" says:

We rejoice in God,
maker of heaven and earth,
and in God's covenant of love
which binds us to God and to one another.[6]

What is covenant and why place it in our understanding of the confession of faith? Covenant is the basis of faith relationships. Gustavo Gutiérrez says, of covenant:

The covenant that God makes with the people is a central theme of the Bible... Covenant means mutual belonging and possession... Husband and wife belong to each other. God's promise to Abraham says: "I will give to you and your descendants the land...and I will be their God" (Gen. 17:8). The love God offers is faithful, but it requires in return a fidelity to the covenant that will seek...justice and right. Love is the foundation.[7]

The confession is not just a personal faith expression. It is not an invitation to a private religious experience. Certainly it changes individuals. "There is," says Gutiérrez, "always the temptation to understand faith as something purely individual."[8] That would make us accountable only to ourselves even though we claim accountability to God. Covenant says that we live out our accountability to God through being part of a mutual, covenantal community. The confession affects the ways individuals take part in the church, the community of faith. This will be discussed in more detail later, but we need to say here that when one makes the confession, if it is taken seriously, it will affect that person's participation in the whole community of faith.

Into What Kind of World Do We Bring This Understanding of Jesus Christ?

It was reported recently that a celebrity said with astonishment, "Jesus is really big now. I wonder why?" Given movies, best-selling serial novels, and the popularity of self-centered spiritual experiences that try not to look denominationally or even theologically traditional, why wouldn't he be "big these days"? Jesus is *in*. But he's also pretty tame, isn't he? Our culture generally favors a nice, safe Jesus. He's "cooler" this way.

In our time resistance to the real call of the confession and its meaning has taken the form of capturing and taming Jesus. We want a Jesus who doesn't ask too much of us—that is, we can't afford him to, if we're going to be affluent, comfortable, self-actualizing, and all the other things in which folks appear to place great importance. As one analyst of the times puts it, we need a "celebrity Jesus," one who can also be called "best friend" and "good teacher"—a nice, attractive, unthreatening, and, for some, patriotic fellow, whose teachings can be shaped to sound a lot like what we already believe.

If that old bottom line of the almighty dollar, inflated though it is, is still the biggest line for most, then Jesus cannot be messing over things like how we spend our money, or whether we practice racism, can he? If we're really going to take care of our self-interest, then he has no business talking about greed and sacrifice and such. So a "big-these-days Jesus" is pretty likely to be a tame Jesus, a Jesus we can pick and choose. We do not particularly like Jesus to tell us how to live our lives, so he becomes a friendly advisor who smiles and lets us stay in charge.

Who, Though, Is This Lord and Savior—Really?

How ready are we to know? We call him Lord, Lord, but does it reach deeper than words and rituals?

A rabbi friend told me years ago about the Hebrew concept of salvation. It comes from the sound that we hear in English as "*schwa.*"[9] The nearest meaning in English is "broad land or space." So when Moses met God speaking from a burning bush on the holy mountain, he heard God say, "I have observed the misery of my people who are in Egypt; I have heard their cry... I know their sufferings, and I have come down to deliver them from the Egyptians, and to bring them up out of that land to a good and broad land, a land flowing with milk and honey" (Ex. 3:7–8).

We know that Canaan is not very wide, but compared to the very narrow valley of the Nile where the Hebrews had to make bricks with no straw, Canaan is a "broad land." For them to be saved was to be taken to a broad place, to be given space, room—in the words of the old Western ballad: "land, lots of land."

The name of the one who finally led them into this "broad space" was *Ye-shua,* or "the one who leads us to a broad place." It is no coincidence that 1200 years later another came who led people to the salvation of broad places, and his name was also *Ye-shua,* or, in Greek, *Iesus,* and in English, Jesus.

Salvation means being led from the tiny prisons we create for ourselves and each other by our alienation and indifference.

This means prisons such as violence, meanness, self-obsessions, blaming, greed, and racism. Jesus leads us from these by showing us that, in God's eyes, we are more valuable than these tiny places. God will do anything to tell us this.

The Gospel for the "Collective"

There remains one critical part to this gospel, and that is that this is not only personal, one-at-a-time; rather, it is collective, not just the faith of rugged individualism, but the life together of the people of God. Jesus Christ is not only *my* Savior, he is *our* Savior. Together we are more than the sum of our parts. As we have already mentioned, the late theologian Letty Russell talked about this when she reflected on the synergy of two or more of us coming together and becoming a new being.[10] Synergy is the "something" that makes us more than the sum of our parts. Faith calls this the Holy Spirit. Jesus Christ not only leads us to smash the personal cages we make for ourselves, but he shows us that racism, sexism, heterosexism, ageism, meanness, addiction to violence, and "my way or the highway" thinking are all abject human failures, ways of making our self-made cages stronger. This synergy is what makes the covenant a living entity and not just a nice concept. A covenantal community, the community that we know as church, is a living organism with processes that are just as alive as those in the individual biological being.

It is the love and grace of God, lived out overwhelmingly in Jesus Christ, that reminds us that we are better than this, and that God deems us so.

What does this mean as we address racism in this new century, this new time in the life of the Christian Church (Disciples of Christ)? It certainly calls us to apply confessional and covenantal thinking and living to the ways we have dealt and are dealing with race, in our personal lives and in our collective life together as a people of faith.

Some painful pitfalls can easily trap us, just as the Egyptians had the children of Israel enslaved in the valley of the Nile. In our time perhaps the most difficult of these is indifference.

To understand this problem we need to remember that we are not living in the Ku Klux Klan–driven U.S.A. In the early part of the twentieth century there were an estimated 3 million members of the Klan, with active organizations in every state.[11] Politics in local, state, and national governing bodies was premised on the "separate but equal" doctrine affirmed in the Supreme Court's *Plessy vs. Ferguson* decision of 1896.

This, however, changed. That change began with *Brown vs. Board of Education* (1954) when the Supreme Court overturned its own earlier decision that had made separation the law of the land. The landscape was altered considerably with the end of separation in schools, housing, voting rights, and public accommodations through civil rights laws in the 1960s.

But the laws didn't eliminate racism. While they banned its public practice, racism went underground. In 2008 hate crimes are still a reality. The events of Jena, Louisiana, are an all-too-fresh reminder of what hate-filled discrimination was like for over 400 years.

Faced with this now-subtle racism, how do people of faith respond?

Many have sought to deal with racism by simply addressing the needs of the victims of this terrible sin. Innumerable faith-based efforts have been made to alleviate ailments such as hunger, housing discrimination, and educational inequities, with most of them assuming that the best way to address racism is to alleviate its consequences. After all, racism does hurt people of color. A primary visible result of racism is the pain and often death it brings to people who do not have white skins. These healing steps are often needed. Because racism often deprives people of color of justice, it can cost them health and well-being. It is important to address these consequences.

It is true, though, that this kind of response to racism, when it is the only one made, can be a good place to hide. I am reminded of a member of a city council several decades ago. When confronted by very angry African American community leaders, he said, "I don't understand want you want. We've done so much for you." Without begging the question of whether that community had done very much at all, the point is they could do everything for those African Americans and it still would not eradicate the racism that was battering and eating at the hearts of those expressing anger that day.

It is, though, so easy to allow indifference to blind us to the reality of racism's power to perpetuate itself, and one of the easiest ways for this to live is when we take solace in our good works.

The confession of faith is also, said Walter Scott, a "repentance of sin," the second finger in that five-finger exercise. Though our founders were, to some degree, trapped in the norms and values of their time, they were still open to acknowledging any of their actions and behaviors as contrary to God's just will.

When we make the confession of faith, with all that it means, can we do any less? And in so confessing, it becomes important to name racism as a sin that has trapped many of us as individuals and collectively.

"We believe that Jesus is the Christ, the Son of the Living God, and we accept Jesus Christ as Lord and Savior."

Some Questions for Reflection and Study

1. What does the confession of faith mean to you?
2. How can the Disciples of Christ be satisfied with the confession of faith as our only "test of fellowship"?
3. How does the confession of faith invite and urge us to confess sins?
4. How is racism a sin? If you do not believe it is a sin, why not?

5. How do we avoid facing racism by only helping its victims?
6. How can your congregation work to confess and then address the sin of racism—in both the congregation and community?
7. Is it necessary to overcome all marks of racism in the congregation before addressing racism in the community?

CHAPTER 5

The Open and Inclusive Table

From our earliest frontier days, the weekly celebration of the Lord's Supper has been a core value for the Disciples of Christ. Though the openness of the table for all who claimed to be Christian was in question for some decades, the absence of human decisions about who could participate in this memorial meal was a common characteristic from the beginning. All parties agreed that no one had the right to bar any believer from the table.

With some differences resolved, and some continuing, over time the table has been generally inclusive to all who "examine [themselves], and only then eat of the bread and drink of the cup" (1 Cor. 11:28). What does this table signify for Disciples?

One refreshingly brisk spring afternoon my wife and I had a picnic on Assateague Island, a national seashore and one of our favorite beach places. We live only a few miles away. We went with our son Ben and his family—Stephanie, his wife, Waylon (then their only little boy), and two dog pets. We were there with wild ponies and sika deer, both miniature and different. It was the first day just warm enough for this outing, and we had a wonderful time. Picnics are that way.

When I was a child of missionary parents in the Congo, several times a year we'd get in dugout canoes and paddle to Iyokompole, a small stream entering the Momboyo River, where, in low water seasons, a long sandbar would come up and we'd just have the best of times. Picnics *are* that way!

In 1801 people gathered, from six states some said, at Cane Ridge Meeting House, in Bourbon County, Kentucky. There they worshiped, testified, celebrated communion, and had what for some was a life-changing week-long revival—much of it, perhaps, like a *picnic*. But this was more than a picnic. It was a time to call people to repentance and a new relationship with God. Unlike other paths to salvation of the time, though, at this great revival people responded personally to God and their faithfulness did not have to be sanctioned by a human religious authority.

This was part of the Great Revival in the West, with four-to-six-day "sacramental meetings" such as this one, based on a traditional Scottish Presbyterian format that focused on the sacrament on the third day. This meeting generated a spiritual fervor and freedom that seemed to some unprecedented in the young nation. With this there came to many a millennial expectation, that is, of the prophesied thousand-year reign of Christ on earth. As a result the event, for some, contained a growing sentiment for social change, particularly the eradication of slavery. The open table might also have been an outgrowth of this sense of God's even treatment and care for all.[1]

Picnics are sharing times, bread-breaking events, occasions to be grateful. At picnics barriers come down and all seem to become one. They are somehow like those wondrous occasions in the gospels when Jesus fed multitudes and all ate the same food.

Yet picnics are not times when people necessarily change. So, while this frontier event may for some have had the inclusive character of a picnic, it was more. It was this community that hosted that great weeklong revival at Cane Ridge that later gave birth to our movement.

The Lord's Supper in Disciples History

The weekly Lord's Supper was among the important early practices of those Christians and Disciples on the frontier. It was first done because they were committed to restoring the New Testament church and it was their conclusion, based on their reading of the Acts of the Apostles (2:46; 20:7) and Paul's letters, that early Christians celebrated the Supper each time they came together, in memory of Jesus' final supper with his disciples.

The frequency hasn't changed, but as much as any other part of our life, the meaning of this weekly observance *has* changed. From a simple memorial meal to a living experience of the presence of Jesus Christ; from a meal meant only for the "pious immersed" to an open and inclusive meal for all who wish to partake and need to be spiritually nourished; it has changed.

Our two most prominent founders, Barton Stone and Alexander Campbell, didn't fully agree on the Lord's Supper. To be at some odds with each other was not unusual for them. In fact, some of their followers were in greater accord that their leaders and were some of the most active in the joining of their respective movements in 1832, notably John Smith, a Kentucky-based colleague who represented the Campbell Disciples in this important joining.

Their difference didn't keep them from uniting. This was one of the early formal occasions where the breadth of the Stone-Campbell experience can be seen. That is, the movement was inclusive of great varieties of belief, a characteristic due in great part to the simple, non-creedal character of the movement.

In his extensive theological work *The Christian System* (1835), Alexander Campbell gave his definitive exposition of the Lord's Supper. He believed that the Supper is commemorative in character and he contended that it belonged to the whole community of believers. His argument was offered in these seven statements:

1. there is a house on earth called the house of God;
2. in the house of God there is the table of the Lord;
3. on that table there is of necessity but one loaf;
4. since all Christians are priests, they all may partake of that loaf;
5. the one loaf must be visibly broken before the saints feed on it (and after giving thanks for it);
6. the breaking of the loaf and the drinking of the cup commemorate the Lord's death; and
7. the Supper is an instituted part of the worship of all Christian assemblies in all their stated meetings (i.e., times of formal worship).[2]

Though he spoke for a Lord's Supper for all, Alexander Campbell was for some time something of an advocate for a Supper that would include only the immersed.

Stone believed in a more open practice of communion. In time Campbell would include the "pious unimmersed"—that is, Christians who hadn't been baptized by total immersion. Yet in some ways it was the experiences of the Campbells more than Stone that opened the door for this meal to become, in time, a wholly open one for all who choose to partake. Alexander Campbell had seen a "fenced" table, one that presumed to keep some from the Supper for reasons given by humans, and he "decried sectarians who fenced each other from the table for doctrinal or political reasons," yet in the mid-1830s he repudiated open communion as "making void" the precedents of the early church."[3] While both Campbells, like Stone, believed a fenced table to be inconsistent with God's desire, Alexander went back and forth for several decades on the matter of open and closed communion for the "pious unimmersed."

Though they established a rather formal, somber observance, the seeds for an open and inclusive table were being planted even as they solemnly partook.

Mark Toulouse, in his book *Joined in Discipleship,* helps us understand this. The concept of the Lord's Supper as a *memorial* was essential to our early history. (In fact, Alexander Campbell called it "the monumental table.") But the Greek word *anamnesis* is the New Testament word for "memorial," and this word means more than simply a memory of something past. In Toulouse's words, it means "the past [is] collapsed into the present."[4]

Another way to say it is that *the Lord's Supper is not just about something that happened, it is about something that is happening.* This memorial is a time when grace is transmitted from out there to in here. And who are we to decide who will receive God's grace?

Yes, we remember Jesus and the Last Supper with the disciples. We can never forget this, nor forget its importance to us as his living body. Blowers and Lambert speak of a shift toward a "eucharistic presence" beginning as early as the mid-nineteenth century, with people sensing a much more subjective reality than the "objective benefits" suggested by Alexander Campbell.[5]

Today, then, we reclaim Jesus; he is alive and present in a powerful spiritual sense, even though the bread and cup aren't actually transformed into his flesh and blood. They don't have to be thus transformed for him to be present. Jesus doesn't need for this to happen, because they *re-present* him to us. For simple elements such as bread and juice or wine to become re-presenters of Jesus Christ means that even you and I can be changed to re-present him to others. That is the real mystery of this amazing table. And our history with it is why it is one of the covenantal values we lift up in this season.

In re-presenting him to us, these elements become the means by which all who will come can receive God's gracious love.

Furthermore, we can never forget the community into which we are called at the Lord's table.

> You, my beloved, once an alien, are now a citizen of heaven: once a stranger, are now brought home to the family of God. You have owned my Lord as your Lord, my people as your people.

Under Jesus the Messiah we are one. Mutually embraced in the everlasting arms, I embrace you in mine: your sorrows shall be my sorrows, and your joys my joys.

Joint debtors to the favor of God and the love of Jesus, we shall jointly suffer with him, that we may jointly reign with him.

Let us, then, renew our strength, remember our Sovereign, and hold fast our boasted hope unshaken to the end.[6]

So, Who Comes?

Douglas Meeks, biblical scholar and teacher, points out that hospitality is one of the five rules of Torah (the Hebrew commandments).[7]

On a trip to the Congo I wanted to find out why the Disciples church there has grown so much. It is some contrast: we Disciples here in North American wonder why our numbers have dropped as they have, while in the Congo they have grown from 250,000 over forty years ago when the United Christian Missionary Society yielded authority to the indigenous church, to over 650,000 today. The Congo has more active Disciples than any other country in the world. I needed to find out: *why?* How could a people beset by poverty, war, and general exploitation be so profoundly committed to evangelism?

Answers came quickly, and the most important was *hospitality*. African culture is hospitable. Just as in the Bible, in which Abram and Sarah welcomed total strangers who, it turned out, were angels (Gen. 18:1–15, Heb. 13:1–2), Africans welcome without hesitation. There they say, "*You* honor *us* by coming into our home," while here we say, "*We* honor *you* by bringing you into our home." In that world they say, "Welcome. Be at home. It is your home." In the Western world we say, "Welcome, but take off your shoes so you won't damage the carpet." There they say, "What's ours is yours." Here we say, "Handle with care, don't break it!"

I lived for three weeks in Kinshasa with the Rev. Ekeya Njali and his family, during which time several families and individuals moved into and out of the house. He did not always know who they were, but they were always welcome.

For them life is too precious to hold onto it in a greedy way. Hospitality rules. Hospitality is why the church has grown so remarkably. Hospitality is not a program. It's a way of being; God's way of being, and it is being practiced there by the poorest of the poor.

So who comes? The lost. The least. The hopeless. The homeless. Even the rich. The poor. The sad. The embattled. Christly hospitality sets up no barriers. If we are to take Paul seriously, then we must say that it is between the individual worshiper and God about whether to eat the food at this feast. We have no choice; we are to welcome whoever comes and even go out and invite them in.

Shaping All Aspects of Our Lives

Everything we do as church can only be done in utter hospitality. As a congregation we are called to practice hospitality to those of all racial, age, economic, ability, and theological groups—and all sexual orientations. We fail God when we make only one or two of these the measure of our hospitality. The vision of our congregations must be open to those battered by racism, ageism, economic injustice, and all the other ailments of a wounded world.

This table has a very loud and eloquent voice that must be heard in all aspects of our lives together and our witness in the world. This table must shape everything we do as congregations and as a Movement. It is no coincidence that in First Corinthians, right after he discusses the Last Supper, Paul begins talking about what it means to be the body of Christ: "Now you are the body of Christ and individually members of it" (1 Cor. 12:27). To be at this welcome table means to be a whole body, inclusive of every part of God's beloved creation.

Called, as Well, to Accountability

If we follow John's description of the Last Supper closely, we have to see that Jesus was really trying to bind his followers together into a community of deep mutual commitment. We use the word *accountability* a lot in conversations these days concerning the church. I understand this word to mean we are to hold each other responsible for being disciples. We answer not only to God but to each other.

In 2005, just a few weeks before the General Assembly in Portland, Oregon, where I had a major leadership role, I had a lesson in what this means. Helping our son build a shed, I missed a step on the ladder and landed ungracefully on my back. It hurt. My lower back and head felt like they had been hit by a truck. The family kept me down and called the ambulance. Two very competent EMTs helped me know that I wasn't in danger of being paralyzed. They invited me to sit, then stand, then decide if I wanted to go to the Emergency Room. I decided to be big and tough and make it on my own. That night, after a day of a lot of pain and being unable to be myself, I had a conversation with one of those visitors who come in the night, who urged me to consider that being tough was not very faithful to the church, and that if I was going to practice accountability to our collective life together, I needed to go be examined for injuries.

The greatest gain from all of this was not finding out that my back was not broken, nor my brains more scrambled than previously, but realizing that I do not belong fully to myself. If this is true, then we never walk alone. We have to answer to God and each other. This is what he wanted his disciples to know that night. He told them so at the table and he wants his Disciples to know today as well. He said, "I give you a new commandment, that you love one another" (Jn. 13:34a). His death for us was not just a sweet syrupy event; it was the ultimate act of accountability, his to God and to us. Let us follow this as we seek to be the beloved community. Are we willing and able to apply this mandate to the eradication of institutional racism in our congregations and communities?

What Is This Table?

It is God's table. Jesus Christ is the host. We may set it, pray over it, serve it, and clean it, but it is God's table. This is God's feast, and God can invite anyone whom God chooses to eat here. We don't know all those whom God chooses to invite, but in our not-knowing, we become committed to welcoming all who come, for each is as important to God as the supposedly most important of us. Even as it gives us the nourishment of spirit that carries us, this meal is the equalizer. Here we are called to be accountable to God and each other, and here we come to examine ourselves to see if we are ready. But here, as well, none of us can judge any other as less than fit to take part if this is what that person, in dialogue with God, is led to do.

When I am partaking of the Lord's Supper, I often visualize myself as a boy, standing at a chin-high wall. I must get on tiptoes to see over very well. On the other side is a great feast spread for all of God's guests, much like the feasts that were had at the mission stations of my childhood in the Congo. The people would come with children, dogs, goats, and the wonderful local food: banganju, bingwele, and bosaka. This is God's final, eternal meal. I don't know all who are there. That's up to God. Someone sees me, comes over to the wall, reaches across and gives me a bite of food. While I'm not ready yet to cross that wall and join the ongoing feast, still, to have a taste and see God's future in the present is a most amazing experience. This is the Lord's Supper, and the feast is open to all God invites.

Some Questions for Reflection and Study

1. Why do we celebrate the Lord's Supper each Sunday in worship?
2. What does the Lord's Supper mean to you and to our whole church?

3. How can the open table of the Lord's Supper be applied to all aspects of the life of your congregation?
4. Do we really love each other? Does that love end at our doors?
5. What would it mean for us to really be accountable to one another?
6. How can our church truly become a place of hospitality in our community?

CHAPTER 6

God's Call to All

While I was experiencing a growing call to ministry, my best friend was called to become a schoolteacher and administrator. By God's grace both of us were able to say "yes" to these vocations, and we have spent our lives in them. They have been quite fulfilling for both of us.

The word *vocation* is rooted in the Latin verb *"vocare,"* or "to call." It can apply to a phone call, being called to dinner, being called on the carpet for whatever, or being called into a particular form of lifetime service. As Disciples of Christ, we have always held to the belief that every person, no matter what other "calls" are on her or his life, is called to ministry for Jesus Christ.

Spiritual Gifts

The ministry of all believers is based on the biblical truth that God places spiritual gifts in all who believe, and places a call to ministry upon every one.

In several places in the New Testament we can see extensive discussions of spiritual gifts, or *"charismata."* Paul and other leaders believed very certainly that God gives gifts to *all* believing followers of Christ. They are to be used for "the work of ministry, for building up the body of Christ" (Eph. 4:12). All people are *not* given the same gifts. Ephesians tells us, "The gifts he gave were that some would be apostles, some prophets, some evangelists, some pastors and teachers" (4:11). Unlike world-wise folk like us, I think that the first readers of these words did not place differing values on those different gifts. All spiritual gifts were of the same worth, because all were given by God. One of the great Christian mystics was Teresa of Avila, who lived in the sixteenth century, and whose experiences of the holy and insights into faith were remarkable. Yet it is said that she believed one of her important gifts was going to the convent kitchen to help clean up. An informal name for her was "the little sister of pots and pans." For her, this was an important way to contribute to the community.

The New Testament lists a number of gifts: being apostles, prophets, evangelists, preachers, teachers; the utterance of wisdom and of knowledge; healing; tongues; the interpretation of tongues; spirituality; leadership; and giving, to name some. There is a clear indication, however, that these aren't the only gifts God gives. It is not ours to choose the gifts God gives us through the Holy Spirit. There are many, many gifts. God gives them and we are called to use the gifts we receive. Nor is the Bible specific about when these are received. They may be gifts by birth, inheritance, training, interest, or a moment of spiritual awakening. All have gifts to be used in ministry.

The Priesthood of All Believers and the Disciples

Our Christian and Disciples founders believed in, and sought to practice, the Protestant Reformation's concept of the priesthood of all believers: "If there is one thing that the first generation bequeathed to the remainder of Disciples history, it is the importance of the laity and its role in ministry. This emphasis grew from the natural soil of the frontier. The ethos of those days...naturally encouraged the development of leaders from among the people."[1]

Early reformers, such as Luther and Calvin, had lifted this up in contrast to the appalling corruption they found in the exclusive, even "clubby" priesthood in the church of their time. Such power as the priests wielded was not by God's will, they believed. Priestly power had become horribly warped in the church. Priests were often not being priestly at all. Thus, the reformers said, all Christians can be priests to one another.

Stone-Campbell leaders agreed: "Campbell's theology of baptism emphasized that every Christian, once baptized, became a minister...and he held that ministry for the congregation arose from among the laity."[2] They found the religious leadership of their time to sometimes be arrogant, insisting that people believe as they, or their tradition, dictated, and this eliminated the laity from any significant role.

As a young minister in preparation, Barton Stone came to believe that the Bible was sufficient; it was all we needed. At his ordination into the Presbyterian ministry he was asked if he could follow the Westminster Confession of Faith. He replied, "So long as I find it consistent with the Word of God."[3]

Of course, those ordaining him believed the Confession was perfectly consistent with God's Word, so they had no problem with Stone's pledge. But Stone, because of his commitment to the biblical guidance he cherished for the church and his mistrust of human authority, had left himself what we might today call some "wiggle room."

It is because of this space that we look today at the ministry of all believers as one of the most basic values of Disciples—past and present.

This "wiggle room" (and Stone could have understood this term) was pretty consistent with a frontier suspicion of authority. The European-descended folks who went West were not the cream of the Eastern seaboard social crop. Wealthy industrialists, great land barons, important bishops, and learned scholars were not the kind of folks who went West. The settlers of this land that was new to them were essentially people wanting a fresh start, people who had been in the lower economic classes back in the East. Many, like the Campbells, came directly from Europe to the West, seeking freedom and unimpeded life and opportunity. As I have mentioned, my great, great-grandfather and his family went from eastern Carolina to western Kentucky, where he died in 1839, for one core reason: to farm *as they pleased, and where they wanted.*

It would have been surprising if those folks had even a moderate level of trust for authority. The frontier era was a time of heady individualism, when "truth no longer emanated from the top down; rather it arose from the will and understanding of the common people."[4]

It would have been more surprising, therefore, if there had *not* been a good degree of anti-clericalism. After all, the East Coast still had some establishment churches—a few, even, that received some public funds. Not on your life would this happen on the Western frontier. The Christians and Disciples in the Stone and Campbell movements were right at the center of this independent mood.

The Place of the One Set Apart for Ministry

In resisting this concentration of spiritual authority, Disciples became notably anti-clerical. There were few clergy in the first fifty years of this frontier movement. It wasn't that the founders didn't feel there was a place for clergy. There just weren't many, and they managed to get along without them. Lay elders led congregations. Mark Toulouse asks an important question about authority concerns in the church's life even today: "Does affirmation of the 'priesthood of the believer,' a treasured concept for Disciples and the whole Protestant reformed tradition, guarantee all Christians the right, at all times, to serve as ministers of word and sacrament in the life of the church?" Toulouse goes on to reflect on one founder's response: "Campbell did not think so. He did, however, assert the right of congregations to assign these responsibilities to lay people 'when circumstances demand it.'"[5] When Disciples did set some apart for pastoral roles, they shared authority with the elders.

In 1865 the first formal education for ministers began at the College of the Bible, part of Transylvania University, in Lexington, Kentucky. Even so, in most of Disciples history the role of the ordained minister has never been exclusive. Ministerial ordination for Disciples does not mean setting a person apart to do special deeds that no one else can do. Rather, it means setting a person apart to do certain deeds in special ways that are shaped by spiritual gifts, education, and choices, not by some mystical authority of office. Park Avenue Christian Church in New York City, to cite one example, has several ordained ministers who are members and all of them are assigned to the eldership of the church. That is appropriate. And while they have certain leadership roles, this doesn't make Richard, Judith, Carlos, Alvin, or any of the others any more spiritual and ministerial than other elders, or even other members for that matter.

As we move deep into the twenty-first century, we have come, with Alexander Campbell, to believe that all are ordained to ministry at their baptisms. All, Paul says, are "given the manifestation of the Spirit for the common good" (1 Cor. 12:7).

As I said earlier, there are no volunteers, only disciples. This means we are *all under discipline* to follow Jesus and to be his servant ministers. This leaves us no way out of service. No one can say, "I'm not as spiritual as Mr. Good or Ms. Nice over there, so I can't do this." I repeat: there is no way out. There is a call on each and every one of us to be ministers or servants of, for, and with Jesus Christ.

All Disciples Are Called to Be Servant Leaders

It was, literally, Mr. I.O. Good who taught me what believing that all disciples are called to be servant leaders really means. Mr. Good was a beloved and highly trusted elder of First Christian Church, Alexandria, where I served as pastor for twenty years. A retired postal inspector, Mr. Good told me at times that he used to believe he had missed his calling. Perhaps, he thought, he should have been an ordained minister. He had come to see, though, that he really had not missed it; he saw himself as a minister, ordination having nothing to do with it. I found out why. Sometimes after worship he would say to me, "Chris, that sermon was pretty good, *but you've got to preach to us that we are **all** leaders. We can't leave it all up to you. If all of us don't lead in this world, then the church might as well close down. We are **all** ministers.*" On many of those occasions his zeal for Christian leadership certainly exceeded mine. What more powerful statement could be made about the ministry of each and every one of us?

Because of their servant leadership, I grew to have high respect for people such as Betty, who was a financial analyst at Housing and Urban Development, and who believed that her ministry was to be certain that people got a fair shake in housing; for Ray, who was an engineer with the Government Services Administration, and who was committed to the maximum use of space in federal buildings so people could do their best work for the nation and not waste resources; for Sue, whose training as a lawyer was being well-used in the Department of Labor, where she was an internal advocate for people who normally got walked on by big business; and for her spouse Bill, a nuclear scientist who, after having served on a nuclear submarine with the U.S. Navy, put on hip boots and slogged through toxic waste sites, cleaning them for the Environmental Protection Agency. Bill was later compelled to change vocations and he became a high school science teacher. He has since died, from cancer likely incurred in those toxic swamps. I could name many more people whose vocations were and are just as vital as mine, people who take Christian ministry seriously enough to run high risks.

The work of leaders in the church is vital. There is no doubt that the church of today can't function without pastors and other designated "ecclesiastical" leaders in its life. Even so, we need to know that Disciples belief says that there is not a whole lot that I can do that lay leaders cannot also do. It is no accident that, as time has passed, Disciples have developed more and more ways for those not formally ordained to assume leadership in the church. The difficulty of this is that the church has a seductive way of making us feel that our leadership roles within the church are what God primarily wants us to be doing.

Yet it is when we all know that our vocations are serious points of ministry that God's work is really done on earth. All too often the number of leader roles within the church drains the energy and commitment of Disciples and we place less value on our leadership responsibilities "out there," in the world, than on those "in here," in the church. If that's the case, we have it backwards and upside down, and only pineapple upside-down cake is *supposed* to be that way. In no case is this opportunity for ministry, in and out of the church, more evident in our time than in the dismantling of racism.

Servant Leaders and Racism

Racism can be defined in a broader secular way, as well as theologically. A very powerful way of understanding it is to see racism as what happens when those in power use it and the institutions that wield that power to enforce their prejudices on those without power. Certainly in the United States when white persons abuse the power available in institutions to enforce white superiority over persons of color, then racism is alive and well.

Often we who are white do not even know this is happening. Because of the privilege white skin gives us we do not normally have occasion to think about it. My family and I do not regularly have dinnertime conversations about racism and the advantages it gives us. People of color, however, tell me that they think daily, even hourly, about its effect on them. This disproportionate reality makes this, I believe, an issue of faith concern.

Leonard Lovett offers a religious definition: "Racism is a moral and spiritual problem. It is the perverse worship of the self, rooted in spiritual pride... It is self-definition in its purest form. Self-glorification and arrogant ingratitude constitute the essential notion of sin. Racism is much more than ingratitude. It is itself religion...a decisive act of turning away from God."[6] Both definitions, the secular and the theological, lift up the notion that racism as we know it in the U.S.A. requires whites to place themselves above the "other," though they are not regularly conscious of it. It requires people of color to struggle with the fact that their place in life is "lower" than the "other." If sin can be seen as resulting in either making ourselves more than we are created to be, or less than we are created to be, then racism is deeply embedded as sin, responsible for both sides of this critical dilemma.

The history of racism in the United States is of one race making itself more than others. White superiority has been part and parcel of the human landscape of this nation from the beginning. For generations those who were not white were not considered humans. The United States Constitution (1787) defined what has been know as the 3/5 rule, in which a slave was worth 3/5 of a person.

> Article I, Section 1: Representatives and direct Taxes shall be apportioned among the several States which may be included within this Union, according to their respective Numbers, which shall be determined by adding to the whole Number of free Persons, including those bound to Service for a Term of Years, and excluding Indians not taxed, three fifths of all other Persons [*Modified by Amendment XIV*].[7]

What this meant was that five male slaves were worth three white people, and thus the number of slaves enabled slave-holding states to have more representatives in the U.S. Congress, *even though those slaves could not vote.* Certainly, as noted, the process of amendments to the Constitution modified this. But it is informative to those who, even today, want the Constitution to say exactly what its writers intended it to say, to know that its writers were trapped by the race construct that said all who were not white were not fully human. Do we want to continue to be trapped by the same construct today?

Healing begins with acknowledging the power of racism over much of life in the United States, including life in the church, which Paul Griffin describes: "American racism, as a body of ideas, is a religious confession. Indeed, it is a theological dogma grounded in powerful but distorted Christian understandings of the biblical text." He discusses how American Puritans, for example, "were preeminent in planting in the American mind the racist confession that God had created black people to be forever inferior and subject to all other races."[8]

Indeed, New England laws stated early on that slaves would be those "taken captives in just wars or such strangers as willingly selling themselves or are sold to us" (Article 95 of the Massachusetts Bay Code of Liberties, 1641).[9]

It is historically accurate to note that this New England law preceded Southern colonies' slave codes, and was meant to support a general labor practice, in contrast to the Southern states' justification of slavery to support one basic economy, agriculture. While this fact does not lessen the horrible reality of slavery in all of the American colonies, it does point out the widespread presence of this onerous practice. It existed *throughout the colonies.* This Puritan-centered Bay Code also shows an example of the theological underpinnings that were used to give a rationale for the practice of slavery across the colonies.

Our history is laced with the fact that racism was, to use a term from the world of pottery, "baked into" the psyche and life of our society, long before any of us were born. It is a core part of our heritage, and some of us believe that deep, faithful confession of this sin-sick condition can begin its eradication. What is the relationship of this fact and hope to the theme of "the priesthood of all believers"? It is simply that this step is required of all of us—certainly including those who are ordained, but, indeed, ultimately, every child of God. We can all be ministers of redemption and reconciliation as we wrestle to eradicate racism from our belief and practice as people of faith.

Some Questions for Reflection and Study

1. Why did the Disciples of Christ emphasize the priesthood of all believers? How did we do it?
2. What does ordination mean for the Disciples of Christ?
3. How do you describe a Christian leader? Within the church? In the community?
4. What is the difference between racial prejudice and institutional racism?
5. How can the church work to overcome racism inside and outside the church at the same time?
6. Do we have to be healed in the church before we can be a healing agent outside of the church?

CHAPTER 7

Our Polar Star

Our children and I sometimes played a fantasy game that asked the question: "When in history would you most like to have lived?" Their answers usually depended on what era they were studying in school, so they'd say, "Colonial America," or "Medieval England." Our son came, in time, to *always* say, "The old, wild West" and he continues to verify this in his adulthood, loving Larry McMurtry's books, good country music, and cowboy boots. Me? My time has always been when they sailed old sailing ships. Loving the sea as I do, it is as natural as can be that I would wish for those times when sailors depended on the polar star for their location and direction. No matter the stink, scurvy, lack of showers, and tiny bunks (if they even *had* bunks) on those old vessels, they charted their courses by the polar star.

Christian Unity in the Young Disciples of Christ Movement

Barton Stone used this image to talk about the importance of Christian unity. We do not know how often he said it, but, as related earlier in this book, in his later years (1835) he wrote, in the *Christian Messenger:*

For 32 years of my ministry I have kept in view the unity of Christians as my polar star. For this I have labored, for this suffered reproach, persecution and privation of ease, the loss of friendship, wealth and honor among men.[1]

One of the founders of our church, the Disciples of Christ of the Stone-Campbell Movement, Barton Stone was convinced that Christian union was of primary importance in the life and work of the church. In his autobiography he reflected on the uniting of the Christians (his movement) with the Reformers of Alexander Campbell. Though there were differences, he noted, "This union, irrespective of reproach, I view as the noblest act of my life."[2]

The Campbells and Stone believed that unity would be attained when reasonable people decided that irresolvable theological disputes were done away with, says historian Michael Bollenbaugh.[3] Stone was passionate in his conviction that human opinions had gotten in the way of what God wants, and one of the results was a divided church.

To call *unity* our "polar star" makes it more than important; it is *who we are*. Unknown to Stone at the time, a few years after the "Christian" movement was launched with the *Last Will and Testament of the Springfield Presbytery* in 1804, Thomas Campbell would write, in his *Declaration and Address* of 1809, that "the church of Christ on earth is essentially, intentionally, and constitutionally one." That is a ringing affirmation for Christian unity! It is to be noted that Thomas Campbell didn't say, "The church of Christ on earth *will be* one," he said it "*is* one."

It would be hard to deny that our founders believed in Christian unity based on the unity God has already given us, and that living into this unity has been the primary collective vocation, or calling, of Christians/Disciples, from our earliest times.

Alexander Campbell believed that restoring the form of the New Testament church would result in cutting through all the human stuff that had accumulated over the centuries so that the church could become, as the early church was, *one*. Stone agreed, but held to the notion that reasonable groups could come together when those issues that could not be resolved were simply not allowed to hinder unity.

Their common belief was that this could be done by getting beyond all those human opinions. In this manner they could restore the *one church* of ancient times. That church would be *one...united*.

They were, in this sense, consistent with the political times, in which the new Western states of the young nation talked often with one another about being *united* into one nation. While independence and individualism were part of the *modus operandi* of the times, people knew they had to join with others to be stronger, whether in self-protection, harvesting grain, or being the church. "Stone compared church disunity to the disaster America might have faced had she been politically divided when invaded by enemies. The churches were like factions that turned against themselves rather than against the common enemy. The command of the King was that all unite in 'one body' against the common enemy."[4] Perhaps Stone had in mind the War of 1812 when this very kind of unity had been necessary for the young nation.

Restoring the intended unity of the church has always been at the heart of our collective life. Jesus prayed, "that they [meaning his followers] may be one, even as we [God and Christ] are one" (Jn. 17:22b).

As time passed the church had divided. As stated earlier, the very name of the church the Campbells were part of—the Old-Light Anti-Burgher Seceder Presbyterian Church of Scotland—suggests several divisions, essentially because several someones "had a better way." Admittedly this is an oversimplification, but it still points to the truth. Our founders were certain that such human opinion reduced the church from a powerful witness to a weak, bickering, unfriendly household. Barton Stone held that for the church to be effective in mission it had to be united: "Christian unity was indispensable to the conversion of the world."[5]

The founders' opinion was consistent with the gospel. In addition to John, the letter to the Ephesians has a powerful and eloquent plea for reconciliation and unity in chapter 2. Reflecting, probably, on the unity that had supplanted former divisions between Jewish and Gentile Christians, thus making circumcision no longer a requirement for participation in the faith, the writer says this: "But now in Christ Jesus you who once were far off have been brought near by the blood of Christ. For he is our peace; in his flesh he has made both groups into one and has broken down the dividing wall, that is, the hostility between us" (Eph. 2:13–14).

It would take a real theological stretch of imagination to interpret these New Testament texts as being for anything less than full oneness of people of faith, oneness based on the truth that that oneness already exists in Christ Jesus.

No wonder it is important to Disciples today. It is in our DNA, part of the very definition of who we are.

To Be as They Were or as They Were Called to Become?

There came the time, though, when we had to choose between *unity* and *restoration*. This is an important distinction. We need to hear it clearly.

In the first generation of leaders of this movement, a strong plea had been that it was part of the Reform movement, that is, the reforming of the church based on what Alexander Campbell called "the ancient order of things." Serious questions arose in the next generation about whether this was possible. Mark Toulouse states, "Though inspired and driven by a sincere commitment to divine purposes in history," it is impossible for the church "to completely escape" either its context "(and, therefore, its relative and finite existence in history)," or "its humanity (and, therefore, its sinfulness)."[6]

The questions becomes, then, not, "Do we want to be just as the New Testament church was?" but rather, "Can we possibly be just as that church was?" The impossibility of such an absolute replication leads to an even more pointed question: "Shall we not, then, seek to live as they hoped one day to live?"

This distinction is important: do we try to be who they were, or do we aim for who they felt called to become? If it's the latter, can we maintain the emphasis on the unity that is so important to us?

Was it their reality or their vision that compels us? Can we be at home in Jesus Christ with the assurance that we are being as they would like to have been? Or do we cast our greatest faith toward the impact of God's Word into our already emerging future?

Believing that all can "become" one because God's church is already grounded in the one creation and the one body of Christ, Disciples have chosen *unity* over *restoration*, becoming the one church God calls and creates us to be.

Disciples believe that it is more important to work for the coming together of all people of faith than it is to presume that our current understanding of the restored church should be the guidebook for all.

What does this mean for us in our actions as a church? How does it guide our lives as believers? Or as those who seek a faith and a community of faith?

Called to Be Healers and Uniters, Not Those Who Hurt and Divide

In a way this sounds pretty presumptuous, doesn't it? *We* are going to heal, unite, and make one all that is divided. Well, if we're going to do it, we've got a job facing us. Not, though, if we believe that God has already laid the groundwork for this healed church and creation. The longer we deny God's given unity, saying that unity really matters to us yet not really living into it, the more overwhelming and daunting the task seems and the less trustworthy our intentions.

It's clear that our formative texts and history call us as Disciples to go against the grain of the times. Our times are certainly divisive, yet we cannot assume that ours are the only times when division was more "in vogue" that unity.

- Even as our founders framed our first communities, the young nation was divided over slavery and the treatment of native peoples.
- Soon after that time a massive and terrible civil war tore the nation apart.
- Industry and agriculture became opposing forces.
- Labor and civil rights ripped us up in new ways.

Hardly ever has this land not been divided. Today is no exception. In politics and economics, racially and ideologically, this is a nation divided. Polarized is the word that's often used to describe it. Can a divided church be a uniting presence? We can be this if:

- All of us, congregations and individual followers alike, see the common call and claim of the gospel as being more important that our individual desires and issues.
- We reach out into our communities to bring people together, no matter how far apart they have been (particularly if being far apart simply means not caring for anyone but ourselves).
- We are willing to risk losing our uniqueness as congregations and change our principles of church organization to the larger good of a denomination and an ecumenical church that seeks to be faithful.
- We act on an impulse for unity that calls us far beyond the church, reaching to all of God's creation, knowing that being apostles of unity must mean taking unity all the way—to *all* of creation.

*All of this sounds pretty abstract, idealistic, and theoretical, doesn't it? What does it **really** mean?*

- What would we do if we were to reach into our secular neighborhoods and address the loneliness that is there?

- What would we do if we were asked to be agents of healing between religious communities that have become political enemies?
- What must we do to become agents of reconciliation in a nation still terribly divided by race?

It is easy to say that laws have changed, schools are no longer "separate but equal," and that the voting booth is now available to all citizens. And the election of Barack Obama is an undeniable sign of cultural change. What this does not say is that hate crimes are on the rise. Nooses continue to appear as though placed in visible places by invisible racist demons. Those equal opportunity schools have taken a backward step recently as the Supreme Court ruled against the continuation of lawsuits that mandate integrated school systems in some cities.

Old Bokulaka was the pastor and preacher at Lotumbe, the town of my birth and childhood in the Congo. He would preach very long sermons. My friends and I would squirm, raise our eyebrows, punch each other, stay a step ahead of our Sunday school teacher (at least we thought so), and Pastor Bokulaka would preach (or, we thought, *drone*) on. He could fill forty-five minutes easily. But one Sunday he caught our attention. He had some sticks bundled and tied together, and he got two of the biggest, strongest men in the congregation of 500 to come forward. He had some twelve to fifteen sticks in the bundle and he asked these two to break the bundle. They laughed and grabbed it, and then wrestled with these sticks, never untying them, just trying in every way to break the bundle. They couldn't do it. Then eighty-year-old Bokulaka untied the bundle and broke the sticks, one at a time. It was easy.

His point made, he sat down. In what seemed just an instant the church was more united than it had been in a long time, as people realized not just that it was good to stick together but that to really be united in Jesus Christ we must often deny our own desires, move over, and let God take our lives wherever God wants to take them.

Old pastor Bokulaka's point, though, went deeper than to insist on the worth of sticking together. The bundle was telling us that the unity we seek *already exists*. One of the most important truths of the ecumenical movement is that we do not create a united church, rather we seek to live into the unity God has already created. Paul Crow, long a leader of the Disciples involvement in the ecumenical movement and world, reflects this in discussing the partnership between the Christian Church (Disciples of Christ) and the United Church of Christ: "The UCC and Disciples confessed that they are (not *will be* or even *hope to be* but *are*) 'kindred in Christ, members together of the one, undivided Church of Jesus Christ.'"[7]

In our zeal for unity we have sometimes defined our mission as being, in essence, to carve out the one church to which we are called. The contemporary ecumenical movement has moved to a place beyond that, not because we have any less passion for unity, but because we realize that we cannot, we do not need to, create the unity God has already shaped.

This passion for unity calls us to places even beyond the church's unity as the sole form into which we are called to live. Realizing that God's creation is meant to be one, that it is created in unity in a way far greater than anything we can do or say, we seek to live into the oneness God has already made within the total human family and, indeed, the whole creation.

Dismantling of Racism as an Act of Uniting

It is in this way that the dismantling of racism becomes part of our mission. God did not create racism. It is a sin that humans have crafted and that has brought hatred and division into God's family. Indeed, the ten denominations of the Churches Uniting in Christ, including the Christian Church (Disciples of Christ) have recognized that confronting racism is at the heart of their shared mission.

Racism's evil is seen in the ways Christian theology was distorted to justify it. Paul Griffin describes the way Puritan theology formed and rationalized this belief that racial superiority was right:

> Regarding the doctrine of creation, their central thesis was that God had not created humanity equal. Human beings had been created hierarchically...There were three levels...ranging from the highest to the lowest. "God Almighty in His most holy and wise providence hath so disposed of the condition of mankind as in all times some must be rich, some poor; some high in power and dignity, others mean and in subjugation."[8]

This approach allowed them, says Griffin, to be the first Christians to "build a theological argument that God had created black people innately inferior to other human beings."[9]

This was certainly not biblical. In fact, the only reference to skin color in the scriptures is found in the Song of Solomon, 1:5–6a—"I am black and beautiful, / O daughters of Jerusalem... / Do not gaze at me because I am dark, / because the sun has gazed on me."

Yet that same Puritan theology took Calvinism's doctrine of predestination and wove it into a rationale for slavery. Paul Griffin describes John Winthrop's way, in his "History of New England, 1630–1649" of "skillfully contorting" predestination into "an argument that makes slavery the result of God's eternal decree, established since the creation of the world, rather than a product of the Puritans' own initiative."[10]

This is but a small portion of the extensive treatment early Christian leaders gave to the work of justifying racism and the evil of slavery using the very same faith that argues, in our thinking, against it. It is our calling to capture God's vision and purpose of a world where there are no walls to divide, where we confess our bent to use others and our passion to see all of God's creation free and whole to the end that the unity of God's whole created order becomes "our polar star."

Questions for Reflection and Study

1. Why has Christian unity been "in the blood" of Disciples, our "polar star," since our frontier beginnings?
2. In what ways is your congregation involved in seeking the unity that God has already created?
3. What does it mean to say that God has already created unity? Why, then, don't we already experience it? How have we missed it this much?
4. What does ending racism have to do with living into God's unity?
5. What can we do in our community to carry out the call to unity?

CHAPTER 8

Restoring the Justice of God

Each Easter we celebrate the resurrection with all of its glory. In so doing, though, we must first acknowledge that justice was murdered that Friday. They thought they had justice firmly nailed down, that a *justitia Romana* (Roman justice), would come from Roman rule for all who mattered. They had justice nailed all right, to a cross.

The Matter of Justice and Justice That Matters

Their understanding of justice was that it mattered only for those who mattered—to them. They had no idea that they were really killing justice. Justice got killed because Roman justice was good only for Romans and their collaborators, so this one who was totally just was cruelly murdered. Then, somehow, he came back from death and the world has not been the same since. Injustice has continued, but from that day forward it would always be seen in light of that true justice. In a true way his was the resurrection of justice. Justice, like unity, was not a quality to be created; rather it was a creation of God to be restored.

My friend Wendell Evans had been arrested again. He was just a high school senior. (Of course, there were those who wondered if Wendell, known as Booboo, would ever graduate. Wendell did feel he had more important matters to tend to—like gaining justice for his people.) Booboo was one of the smartest and certainly the most articulate young person I have ever known.

Black and angry, he stuttered with just about every syllable, but few could name their passion about injustice like he could. Booboo lived with his aunt in the projects. We'd come to know each other through an Urban League youth project that our congregation co-sponsored. We walked the streets together during civil unrest, me to somehow say, "Not all white people hate you!" and he to make his nonviolent protest while protecting me from angry African Americans. Now Booboo was in jail, arrested on fake charges, held because those holding him believed he was a danger to the city. He was dangerous all right, because he upset the Jim Crow status quo.

We were able to get the mayor, the minority party city council leader, and a host of others to pool resources and energies to get Booboo out, not to gain some political *status quo* because his jailing would rub some folks as wrong, but just because it was unjust. He had been arrested on obviously bogus charges, and it was simply wrong.

Those were not easy days in that small city in the very shadow of Washington, D.C., yet just below the Mason-Dixon Line. This was the city of later *Remember the Titans*[1] fame, a place often notorious for its unequal justice. Sometimes, though, even there, justice rose and defeated death. Easter's witness is that God's power overcomes death, darkness, evil, meanness, and all the work that evil does to capture us. *God is more powerful!*

But if we are to celebrate the Easters of life in authentic ways, then we need to name and claim the restlessness that Christian people have to feel in this world, which is still so unjust. Poet Marge Piercy speaks of this restlessness, calling it "A just anger":

Anger shines through me
Anger shines through me
I am a burning bush
My rage is a cloud of flame.
My rage is a cloud of flame
in which I walk
seeking justice
like a precipice.
How the streets
of the iron city
flicker, flicker,
and the dirty air fumes.
Anger storms
between me and things,
transfiguring,
transfiguring.
A good anger acted upon
is beautiful as lightning
and swift with power.
A good anger swallowed,
a good anger swallowed
clots the blood
to slime.[2]

Anger it is. Is this not the root of the restlessness that some people of faith have to be feeling in these days when unequal justice spreads its ugly tentacles so widely? We cannot face injustice as an academic subject.

On examining the word *justice,* I found a number of definitions, but the most common word in all of these was "fairness," or equity. The prophet Micah saw it as essential to the salvation of God's people. Folks had come to God with sacrifices for generations. Priests had gone to the altars of the Hebrews and sought God's blessing. People had made burnt offerings that smelled right and were properly lit and so on. Right things had been done, yet the people were no closer to

God than before, and, furthermore, they were so wrapped up in pleasing God to justify themselves personally that they had little concept of and urgency about God's call to reach out and build a just community.

Justice and its necessary practice of fairness for all had been abandoned. Kindness was in short supply. Humility was scorned. The poor were used. The rich became richer. All of this they tried to cover with rituals. Now they were in trouble because they were threatened by greater military powers. Political deal-making was replacing faithful and trusting obedience. So Micah asked and answered his own question, "What does the Lord require of you / but to do justice, to love kindness, / and to walk humbly with your God?" (Mic. 6:8).

Jesus was raised on this prophetic theology. We can't read of him and conclude that he came into adulthood believing that proper sacrifices, dutiful duties, and impressive offerings, all to cover a multitude of self-serving sins, were what mattered the most. Did he have a rabbinic teacher who was unusually sensitive to issues of justice, or did he just pick it up? However it came to him, he was and is *justice* personified.

John's gospel tells us that we will not all see the risen Christ. He said to Thomas, "Have you believed because you have seen me? Blessed are those who have not seen and yet have come to believe" (Jn. 20:29). But what we *will* all see are injustice and justice. And the call is ours to witness to the truth that justice lives because Jesus lives.

Yet people, dare we say even "Christian people," put some pretty self-centered boundaries on justice. In Taylor Branch's great trilogy on America during the Martin Luther King years, the first book is *Parting the Waters*. To me, the most amazing part of this story is how major figures in American life (all of whom always claimed to be people of faith), but politicians in particular, were willing to postpone justice in order to please particular people.[3] It was as though they were saying, "Don't say too much, you might make the southern folks mad." Or,

"Let's do this lunch counter stuff a little bit at a time." In a too-brief interim ministry in the Park Avenue Christian Church, New York, I came to know a quiet man and member, Preston Davis, who, I found out, was one of the very courageous young people who years earlier first engaged in a sit-in in Greensboro, North Carolina. It is an honor to know this man whose willingness, typical of the bold people of the time, eventually resulted in justice in the public arena for countless millions of Americans.

What colossal arrogance it is to put human boundaries on divine justice! What amazing presumption, what monstrous sin, and what an invitation to self-destruction, that we would count some people as of less value than others, notably than ourselves, that we would say, "They can wait until it's convenient."

Yet this is a terrible part of our story, and not just *our* story, but the human story. William Gladstone, the nineteenth-century British statesman, was the likely source of these wise and challenging words, and was so right when he said, "Justice delayed is justice denied."[4] He has been often quoted in this wisdom, a wisdom born of the pain of seeing unequal justice applied again and again by humans against other humans— from London prostitutes (whose "redemption" he took a particular interest in) to those victimized by Great Britain's colonial empire. We proceed now to examine one powerful point of delayed (or ignored) justice.

The Prison-Industrial Complex in the U.S.A.

A vivid contemporary example of justice applied unequally can be found close at hand in what has been called the Prison-Industrial Complex in the United States. Quite frightening statistics are now available about the criminalization and disenfranchisement of people of color in the criminal justice system.

In the late 1960s and into the 1970s, the federal budget put large amounts of money into building airports and providing technical education. Today, while airports and technical education receive far less by comparison, these same funding levels go into the building of prisons. Over the past several decades we have seen an increase in the incarceration rate of men of color. In 1973, 12 percent of young men of color were either incarcerated or otherwise involved with the criminal justice system. This percentage has changed drastically: In 1985 it had grown to 25 percent, in 1995 it had gotten to 33 percent. Robette Ann Dias predicts that 50 percent of young men of color will eventually be involved, in some way, with the criminal justice system.[5]

According to Bureau of Justice statistics, in June 2006 the Department of Justice estimated that 56.1 percent of all inmates in the United States were people of color. Of those, more than 38 percent were African American and more than 15 percent were Hispanics. Only 43.9 percent were Non-Hispanic white inmates. This number is down from June 2005, when 44.3 percent of all inmates were white.[6]

It is impossible to justify this dramatic rate of increase on the basis of increased criminal activity. Men of color would have to be worse than the most criminal elements of history to justify these punishment rates.

One need only look at the unequal sentences for powdered cocaine (predominant in suburban, white, middle-class contexts) and crack cocaine (urban, lower- to middle-class, black or Hispanic contexts) to see this unequal justice at work. One guilty of possession of powdered cocaine will receive a sentence of, at most, a few years, while the crack cocaine possessor may be sentenced to thirty or forty years. This is so appalling that leaders of the criminal justice system have moved to make this sentencing process more equal.

Finally, it is important to be aware that the planners who design the number of prisons that are needed twenty years from now base their calculations on the standardized test scores of fourth graders, under the apparent assumption that those who, right now, aren't being well-served by the educational system will, in the future, be served instead by the prison system.[7]

This raises a most telling question: are standardized tests really done to improve performance and teacher accountability, or to plan for the prison-industrial complex? The latter is so named because prisons are now often managed and staffed by industries, and prisoners are trained in far more sophisticated occupations that making license plates. Note that the next time you receive a phone call from a marketer or call a service technician, the responder may well be a person in an American prison on a felony charge.

Born in Justice

Disciples and Christians were born in a radical setting of justice. No one was higher than anyone else. The ground was leveled for all. God's grace did not come less to any than to all. As a frontier people we were radically egalitarian—which means there was no hierarchy. We were each equally loved by God. Regressive contemporary opinions about the races notwithstanding (and they were certainly there!), this was God's justice. Either God did not create failures or God made all of us failures. It is more likely that God creates no "lemons," but, being free, we wander or plunge into lemon-land on our own initiatives.

We are told in the creation parable in Genesis that God said, "Let us make humankind in our image, according to our likeness; and let them have dominion" (Gen. 1:26). The first striking word after *make* is *our*. A real issue in the struggle to overcome racism is the "me" versus the "we." White people tend to view racism as an individually focused disease, thinking that if we can teach individuals to grow beyond prejudice, we will conquer racism's evil. While it would be nice to enable all white persons to be un-prejudiced, people of color know what a pipe dream that is and what racism really means.

A Collective Evil and a Collective Response

Racism is not an illness confined to individuals. Racism is the collective evil committed when people of one race, their prejudices shaping their actions, put those prejudices together with the abuse and misuse of institutional power, and simply use people of other races in ways that favor those who held to prejudice and power in the first place. People of color say that racism is *not* just individual prejudice; it is the collective power of those in charge that makes it possible to use their institutional might to reinforce their prejudices about various races. This is injustice. Justice, measured by my or our own criteria will always need to be tested against a norm of equal justice for all.

We cannot be independent of one another. "The notion of a distinct and separate 'I' is not mentally, ethically or seriously sound because it conceals the process by which we stand in radical interdependence and mutual re-creation."[8] People question individualism's capacity to sustain itself: "What is at issue is not simply whether self-contained individuals might withdraw from the public square to pursue purely private ends, but whether such individuals are capable of sustaining either a public *or* a private life."[9]

While we may like to idealize rugged individualism, one must question whether it ever really existed. The frontier mentality of America may be more myth than truth, for this nation's frontier was a place where people were far more interdependent than today. For building, plowing, planting, harvesting, self-protection, and in many other times and ways, people banded together. Just as living was a collective activity, so racism is collective.

Consider a notable and terrible example: Eugene "Bull" Conner of Birmingham, Alabama. He had made "Birmingham into his private fiefdom of segregation, with bareknuckled police tactics that had done nothing to discourage a tradition of vigilante violence."[10] Could Conner have wielded such power as a lone individual? Hardly. His own ugly prejudice, coupled with the abusive use he made of the Birmingham police, resulted in fire hoses, police dogs, and other tactics reminiscent of a horrible Nazi state. Was this individual action? No. Insidious work of this kind and scale has never been carried out by people working alone. This was collective action.

It is, further, important to note that the word in Genesis 1:26 is "dominion" and not "domination." Yet the whole human story is one of assuming domination, rather than dominion. We want to run things, not manage them. We want to *use* the creation, not *nurture* it. Moltmann said that the two sins we commit are sins of "arrogance" and sins of "despair."[11] Racism is an act of arrogance, where what we want and believe we need takes precedence.

Can we recover?

The Disciples of Christ have used Micah's prophetic words in 6:8 to name our vision for the coming decades: "To be a faithful, growing church that demonstrates true community, deep Christian spirituality, and a passion for justice."

A Passion for Justice

All of the core-covenantal values we have explored in this text point to justice, or *God's desire to return to all of creation the dignity and life with which all are created.* Walter Brueggemann says, "the justice that is proposed and for which concrete implementation is provided...is a social practice in which the maintenance, dignity, security, and well-being of every member of the community are guarded in concrete ways, and that God's 'preferential option' is for the ordering of neighborly community."[12]

Human history is full of examples of justice applied unequally. The truth that overarches all of this history is that justice cannot be maintained if it is not carried out equally for all. Racism, by its very definition, makes justice unequal. Racism is, therefore, wrong and doomed, finally, to wreck on its own self-delusion.

A Summary of the Covenantal Values

The confession of faith in Jesus Christ, which alone is asked of people as a test of fellowship for this church, the inclusive

Lord's Supper to which all who seek Christ are invited and who cannot be barred from partaking, the ministry of all believers, and the vocation of unity-making are all rooted in God's justice.

Our origins are deep in justice. We have not always practiced what we have preached, but by God's grace we can see justice come to life in fresh ways in our church and, more importantly, beyond. One of the reasons justice has had a hard road to travel has been that we have been satisfied to feel justice within the church, but have not worked too hard to witness for God's justice beyond our walls.

Justice that is applied within the church but isn't taken out to the world is stunted, self-focused, and is really injustice. In all that we do—from evangelism to world mission, lunches for the homeless to day school, new congregation planting to leader training, the arts to being wholly open for all of God's beloved children—in *all* of this, God's justice is required of us. God's justice, again, means returning to all creation the dignity and value with which God creates us.

Some Questions for Reflection and Study

1. What is justice?
2. How would you define and describe God's justice?
3. Why is justice important enough to be named so often in the Bible?
4. Has the church ever been drawn into doing injustice? How?
5. What does it mean to restore God's justice?
6. How can your congregation act to help bring justice to racial life in your community? Or is it just fine the way it is now? If so, how so?

CHAPTER 9

Becoming One

The title of this chapter is not followed by either an exclamation point or a question mark. An exclamation would suggest enthusiasm from tangible and clear progress. A question mark would itself be a statement that we don't know if we have made any progress in this journey, but the opportunity *may* still be there. Are we ready yet to place one of these marks? This chapter will argue that we are not yet there, but there is still time because the opportunity *is* still there.

A Step or Two Forward and One or Two Back

This seems to be our pace these days, one or two steps forward and one or two back. What is different is that the forward steps and the backward steps vary. Progress in one area may be countered by regression in a subtle aspect of that same area, or even in another. Let's look at some examples.

The desegregation of public education in the United States beginning in the 1950s was clearly a step toward justice. The facts that many schools are resegregating and that the Supreme Court recently ended court-ordered desegregation processes in two major city systems, Louisville and Kansas City, seem to many to be backward steps.

The Fair Housing Act of 1968 was a positive and hopeful justice move. There remain, though, significant difficulties for people of color when the time comes to arrange financing for home purchases. There is more access, to be sure, but the time taken for clients of color to go through loan processing can be discouragingly long and made unnecessarily complicated. Quality of life for people of color, as seen in the prison system data (see chapter 8); availability of good shopping places and public transportation; and access to good health care are hardly improved. Listen to the late Arthur Ashe, as he spoke in 1993: "Most blacks seem to agree that the quality of our lives is worse now than ten years ago. It is almost certainly worse than in the 1960s."[1]

Disciples anti-racism teams often lead congregational workshops, and in many we ask participants to compile two lists: one of ways in which race relations have gotten better since the 1960s, another of ways they have gotten worse. In reflecting on these lists a surprising number of people say that these relationships are both better *and* worse.

So the decision between an exclamation point and a question mark remains. We stand on the edge of real gains or tragic losses. How can we move from this place where we so often seem to be stuck?

Becoming a "People"

As was stated in chapter 8, it has been said many times that if we just educate enough people about the terrible price paid due to racism, then we will overcome. Time and again this question has been put to white people and people of color. White people tend to agree, saying, "Let's just get everyone on board and we'll lick it!"

People of color, on the other hand, say that racism is a collective evil. Racism, as we know it, is very often expressed in individual acts of injustice, but the gathered power of systemic racism is a far greater force. At some point the prejudices of the individuals in charge, or of the "majority" mind-set, are put together with manipulated and abused institutional power and the result is a system that is terribly distorted and tilted against all who are not white.

If racism is a collective evil, how can we address it by just trying to change one person at a time? We can only address it as we become a "people," a community of concern. The truth that we gain strength in numbers can certainly be applied to racism's work and to anti-racism's counter-work.

Being "a people" is certainly consistent with the Bible's history and guidance. When the children of Israel came to Mt. Sinai in the desert, after long years of slavery in Egypt, God came to them offering a covenant. God had interacted with individuals before: Adam, Noah, Abraham, Sarah, Isaac, Rebecca, Jacob, and Moses. Now God was interacting with "the people." In no way does this mean God and other individual spokespersons, such as the prophets, did not interact. But it does mean that human understanding of God's primary relation to the human family moved from only a "one to one" basis to a "one to many" framework. Put another way, God did not make covenant only with individual Israelites, God made covenant with "the people of Israel."

It isn't always easy for Disciples to grasp this. We were born and began to grow up on the frontier, where radical individualism was normative. Yet even there people joined for protection, harvests, and revivals (such as Cane Ridge in August of 1801). Were we to have to choose between individual and collective, would there even be an argument? Our congregations are *communities*. Our decisions are made *together*. We do not have to make that choice. We can still be individuals, but we need to know that if racism's evil is made greater by its collective power, then the dismantling of this evil will only come when we act together to address it.

Our faith calls us to act as "a people" and not just as separate individuals who may, at times, pool resources to do some good. In 1 Corinthians 12 Paul talks about the importance of "the body" and the individual parts, or members. The church is the "body of Christ," made up of individual members who, joined together, become a body that could not happen without those various parts.

If we want, then, to be serious about dismantling racism, we need to function as a body, a collective. No matter how many individuals are changed, they will not change an evil that has been collectively imposed until they themselves become a "collective."

Becoming a Proleptic People

Prolepsis, the word from which *proleptic* comes, is defined as "a figure of speech in which a future event is referred to in anticipation."[2]

Prolepsis conveys the idea of being pulled to a place or another goal. It is seen in the ways Jesus talked about the "kingdom of God" as being both "near" (Mt. 4:17) and "today" (Lk. 23:43). In his vision, God's realm was both already present and coming.

Proleptic people of faith, then, are people whose certainty about God's reign is such that we know God's full rule is coming, and, as we move toward it, we become more and more as God wants us to be *when that rule has fully come.* We are not driven to reach that goal in our time. We are captivated, though, by the possibility of that realm's coming, and willing and able to work toward that coming.

When a magnet begins to attract iron filings, they are drawn toward the magnet and the nearer they get to the magnet the greater the magnet's power to attract them. The moment when that movement begins is like the beginning of a proleptic faith.

When people of faith begin to see racism's deceit and the brokenness it brings about, and become convinced that God's sure call is to dismantle racism in all of its evil forms, then a proleptic movement can begin to take place. To become proleptic is, as well, consistent with the character of Disciples. We have never considered ourselves a finished product. Always in process, ever reaching further and further, our prayer could well begin with a plea that God save us from ever becoming so stuck in one place that we will never change.

Becoming a Confessing People

As a usual practice, confession, for Disciples, is private. In liturgy very few congregations have formal times of collective confession, choosing instead to leave that as something between each worshiper and God. (1 Cor. 11:28–32 is an example in which this is applied to one's preparation for the Lord's Supper.)

At the same time, many white persons say, today, "We are not responsible for the racism of the past, and particularly slavery. Don't blame us for our great-grandparents' sins. What is there for us to confess? Let's just get on with living!"

It is true that today's whites did not create the system of slavery that had such a massive place in building the U.S.A. But, at the same time, it is true that white persons today continue to reap the benefits of a system that puts whites on the top of a deceptive racial ladder. James Loewen tells about a conversation with a librarian in Arkansas, who said, "African Americans were the people enslaved. So whites had to make them intellectually inferior to justify enslaving them."[3] While most whites may not consciously feel the legacy of this process that began long years ago, has it ended? Did the Emancipation Proclamation also guarantee that whites would no longer consider themselves superior to persons of color? Did the end of the Civil War or the 14th Amendment to the U.S. Constitution guarantee that former slaves would be immediately considered the intellectual and emotional equals of whites? Of course not.

Where this really comes home to roost for white Americans today is in the reality of privilege. Who has the greater privilege today? Mary Elizabeth Hobgood (a distant cousin of this author) argues that while "the race system, which gives whites dominance over other racialized groups, also restricts whites emotionally and damages us morally...the truth is that whites gain at the expense of communities of color, which is the primary reason for the construction of whiteness and the racial system."[4] The reality of white privilege has been explored by Peggy McIntosh in a paper titled, "White Privilege: Unpacking the Invisible Knapsack." In this provocative work she gives a succinct analysis of white privilege and its roots for individual white persons:

> I think whites are carefully taught not to recognize white privilege, as males are taught not to recognize male privilege. So I have begun in an untutored way to ask what it is like to have white privilege. I have come to see white privilege as an invisible package of unearned assets that I can count on cashing in on each day, but about which I was "meant" to remain oblivious. White privilege is like an invisible weightless knapsack of special provisions, maps, passports, codebooks, visas, clothes, tools and blank checks.
>
> I see a pattern running through the matrix of white privilege, a pattern of assumptions that were passed on to me as a white person. There was one main piece of cultural turf, it was my own turn, and I was among those who could control the turf. My skin color was an asset for any move I was educated to want to make. I could think of myself as belonging in major ways and of making social systems work for me. I could freely disparage, fear, neglect, or be oblivious to anything outside of the dominant cultural forms. Being of the main culture, I could also criticize it fairly freely.[5]

It becomes fairly obvious to sensitive white persons where privilege begins to take a prominent place in our lives. McIntosh gives a long and growing list of such places in her life, and from these whites can readily identify privilege's power in our lives.

"As far as I can tell," she says, "my African American coworkers, friends, and acquaintances with whom I come into daily or frequent contact in this particular line of work cannot count on most of these [following] conditions.

- I can if I wish arrange to be in the company of people of my race most of the time.
- I can avoid spending time with people whom I was trained to mistrust and who have learned to mistrust my kind or me.
- If I should choose to move, I can be pretty sure of renting or purchasing housing in an area which I can afford and in which I would want to live.
- I can be pretty sure that my neighbors in such a location will be neutral or pleasant to me.
- I can go shopping alone most of the time, pretty well assured that I will not be followed or harassed.
- I can turn on the television or open to the front page and see people of my race widely represented.
- When I am told about our national heritage or about 'civilization,' I am shown that people of my color made it what it is."[6]

It is important to note that all of these benefits of privilege are good. They are not nefarious, biased benefits in themselves. The reality is simply that they accrue to whites in an abundance unknown to persons of color. It is this kind of benefit and the truth that whites do receive these in a system designed for it to be this way that call us to confession.

From time to time a white person in an anti-racism workshop will say, "I don't have any power of the kind that racism is built on." That may be true on the surface. There are many whites who do not appear to have economic or political power, for instance, in any major way. But, after exploring an analysis of racism's history and mode of operating, no white person yet has denied the reality of privilege.

Confession will not end collective racism. It can, however, bring about a remarkable benefit. Audrey Smedley points out, "If you give up racism, you're not giving up privileges. What you're doing is expanding privileges."[7] It can, in other words, make white persons sensitive to that which we receive in disproportionate amounts, so we can be better motivated to be sure that *all* persons receive these benefits.

Becoming a Restorationist People

In earlier parts of this book there was discussion of how Disciples on the frontier were committed to the restoration of the early church. Many were convinced that this was what God wanted. Through restoration the church would become accessible to all people who believe in Jesus Christ as Savior, and this would enable all who call themselves Christian to come into unity around the simple propositions of that early church. Restoration as an idea should not be unfamiliar to Disciples.

We need another kind of restoration where dismantling racism is concerned. We need, by God's grace and love, to restore the human community as God intended it to be. God called us to life as family, not as a hierarchical system that puts some over others. God called us into being to live lives of hope, not for some to be first the property of and later the social and cultural doormats for others.

At first hearing, this approach to restoration may seem a backwards one because it uses a concept that has not been particularly relevant for Disciples. By no means is this the case. Walter Brueggemann reminds us, "The justice command [in the Old Testament] witnesses to Yahweh's preferential option for the ordering of a neighborly community."[8] Does not a community include all its members? To restore, then, God's "community" means the inclusion, on level ground (see Isa. 40:3–4), of all of God's beloved creation, as God intended it to be from the beginning.

It is when this approach to "restoration" becomes the goal of people of faith that we see proleptic movement beginning and growing. We do not know how long this movement will last. We can only say that it will take as long as is necessary for community, as God created it, to be restored. The dismantling of racism is at the heart of this movement.

Becoming a People with Memory and Knowledge

Disciples are an informed and intelligent community. Reason has, from the beginning, stood at the soul of our character. How do we apply this to racism that is still alive? "Those who cannot remember the past are condemned to repeat it," said George Santayana, a philosopher/teacher of the early twentieth century.[9] At first hearing this seems so logical. Yet, is it not a human tendency to repeat history time and again? What are most wars if not efforts to either win land or turn back those who want to win land? The weapons we use have changed, but the reasons for war have, sadly, stood the test of time. The lesson is this: we are not very good at remembering the past, learning from history, or using our memories for more than only being repositories of cherished yesterdays.

Disciples, placing significant emphasis on the importance of reason, can learn and remember.

We can remember from our own early story that slaves could worship in balconies and outside the windows of frontier churches and that separate movements for Disciples of color emerged (the Assembly churches—i.e., Churches of Christ/ Disciples of Christ—for example) so as not to undergo the humiliation of racism in church life.

We can remember that the Cherokee Strip Land Rush, to claim land that had been the possession of the already once-dispossessed Cherokee American Indian peoples in Oklahoma, resulted in land claims for several Disciples congregations and the earliest formation of what later became Church Extension.

We can remember that our mission societies, with good intention, carried out major "programs" for children of former slaves across the South, and organized "missionary" congregations among former slaves. The question arises, today, if many recipients found these to be paternalistic, treating

African Americans of all ages like children: "I think that as we look back in history through a different lens than those people, the programs were a both/and [both beneficial and patronizing]"[10] As an outgrowth of all of this racialized history, Preston Taylor and his fellow African American Disciples church persons (as referred to earlier in this book) organized the National Christian Missionary Convention in 1917. It became a continuing national entity of African American Disciples, in part to remove them from the "recipient" role they had held with white Disciples. In time, says Brenda Cardwell, we would come to realize that African American Disciples were "no longer objects of mission, but partners in mission."[11]

Our memories now need to expand beyond the Disciples of Christ.

In the nineteenth century scientists developed what, for that time, was a sophisticated way of determining the inferiority of persons of African descent. Samuel Morton was a scientist who took on the question of skull sizes as denoting differences in races. Josiah Nott, another scientist, took up the cause of polygenism, that is, the belief that black persons were of an entirely different species than whites. Louis Agassiz was a Swiss naturalist who came to America, taught at Harvard, and became a devotee of the polygenists theory of different origins.[12] In truth, "Race in the American collective consciousness had already assumed the same dimensions of differentiation as 'species,' even without a change in the terminology."[13]

The point of all of this is that after the Civil War white people were conditioned to believe that black persons were inherently inferior, that the problem with slavery was the slaves, not the slavers, and that recognition of the inferior status of blacks was essential to survival.

This was affirmed judicially and politically in the 1896 *Plessy vs. Ferguson* ruling of the United States Supreme Court that has already been referred to. The Court ruled that a state (Louisiana, in this case) had the right to regulate the separation of races in railroad cars, as long as they were within the state. The law to that effect had been challenged in an organized effort. What the Court did not take into account in their ruling was the reality that Jim Crow laws were already being passed in many states and localities, mandating separate facilities, most of them unequal. So while *Plessy vs. Ferguson* was in support of "separate but equal," in reality it gave blessing to "separate but unequal," which prevailed in the United States until *Brown vs. Board of Education* ruled it unconstitutional in 1954, and the Civil Rights Act of 1965 required the banning of Jim Crow laws in public facilities.

In many other places racism was, and continues to be, alive and well in this nation. James W. Loewen describes the period from 1890–1930 as "the Nadir" of racism in the U.S., when, even after slavery was over and laws had been passed affirming civil rights, racism was at its mean worst. "Ultimately," he says, "racism is a vestige of 'slavery unwilling to die,' as Supreme Court Justice William O. Douglas famously put it."[14]

What can we say to this? To assume that racism ended in the past is to deny reality. Prison statistics (see chapter 8), the economic differences, and the ease with which undocumented immigrants are (for the first time in history) called "illegal," are but a few examples of the continuation of what Audrey Smedley called the "demonization" of the "Negro" in the nineteenth century.[15]

All of this, to a people of reason and faith, can only point us to a search for a deeper, more faithful way to live life.

Becoming an Outraged People

When I was a small child, a Sunday school teacher told us that Jesus only got angry one time, and that was when he turned over the tables in the temple (Mt. 21:12–13, and in other gospels). We were taught that anger is not good and that if we were going to grow up to try to follow Jesus we should never get angry (unless, I suppose, we find a bunch of money-changers in some temple).

It took a lot of years to begin to read anger in Jesus on other occasions, as when he rebuked Peter, even calling him Satan, for Peter's denial of Jesus' discussion of his coming suffering (Mt. 16:21–23); the several times when people tried to keep children away from him; or his challenging replies to scribes and Pharisees, even calling them "blind guides" (Mt. 23:24). Finally, I came to see that Jesus was angry at times, and for good reason.

Paul, or a later follower of his using his name, told the Ephesian Christians, "Be angry but do not sin; do not let the sun go down on your anger" (Eph. 4:26). Anger that is not dealt with is not healthy. But anger, if utilized in fair and caring ways, can be valuable. This is the way Jesus used anger.

Outrage, though, is anger of a deeper, less immediately volatile, yet more lasting kind. The dictionary tells us that outrage as a noun means "abuse, affront, indignity, insult, or offense."[16] It is not too much to call Disciples—who have heard and seen, listened and read, prayed and struggled to understand racism's sinful work—to a level of outrage that will result in doing something about it. In an old comic strip, Snuffy Smiff's wife Loweezy storms out of the house with an axe, saying, "Snuffy, you told me you were going to chop that stump out of the yard. Here's the axe." Snuffy, taking a snooze as he lay against the stump, replied, "I'm gonna lean it out, woman!"

Racism cannot be leaned out. It cannot be dismantled gently, a bit at a time. To eradicate it requires all the elements discussed in this chapter *and* a deep sense of outrage about what it has done again and again to God's beloved children. But again, we have to remember, racism's purpose is not to kill, hurt, or even harm people of color. Rather it is to bring benefits to white persons and then to keep these coming.

We need, therefore, to be smart with our sense of outrage. It is difficult to find a better example of intelligent use of outrage that Dr. Martin Luther King's *Letter from the Birmingham Jail.* Imprisoned during the Birmingham demonstrations of 1963, King responded to a story in the *Birmingham News* in which eight white clergymen, all "at least mild critics of segregation," issued a statement calling the Birmingham Campaign that Dr. King led "unwise and untimely."

King's response, written in margins of newspaper pages and on any paper he could find, is a masterpiece of moral prose. He says, "Shallow understanding from people of good will is more frustrating than absolute misunderstanding from people of ill will." "One day," he said in his conclusion, "the South will know that when these disinherited children of God sat down at lunch counters, they were in reality standing up for what is best in the American dream and for the most sacred values in our Judaeo-Christian heritage..."[17]

It is this kind of measured but uncompromising response to the evil of racism that God calls us to express.

Becoming a Leadership People

"We are all leaders," said Mr. I.O. Good (see chapter 6). Mr. Good was pointing to a reality that the church has not often accepted: that the church is a body. In terms used in this book, we are a "collective," and though we may not, as individuals, all consider ourselves leaders, together we are called to lead when the time comes to defy racism and dismantle its evil power to misuse institutions:

> To lead is to live dangerously because when...you lead people through difficult change, you challenge what people hold dear—their daily habits, tools, loyalties, and ways of thinking—with nothing more to offer perhaps than a possibility.[18]

Some say the church has been too cautious in facing racism. Dr. Martin Luther King said often that 11:00 a.m. Sunday was the "most segregated hour of the week." That may be so, though it has stiff competition from the hours of 6 p.m. to 6 a.m. in most American homes. Whichever is most accurate, the church has not done well in overcoming the barriers created by racism. Whether Christians still hold to a theology of white supremacy as developed and widely taught in colonial times is debatable, but the fact is Christians have been very slow in establishing the true bonds of community to which we are called in the gospels (Jn. 17:21) and the epistles (Eph. 2:14, 16–18).

How can the church best lead in this most important process of change? There are two critical leadership qualities to be aware of and to use: example and authority.

Few institutions may be more closely watched than the church when issues of morality and justice are concerned. This may seem a grandiose statement in a "post-religious" time, and this is such a time. It seems, though, that the church is observed most closely by those who are eager to criticize and even maul religious groups for their "hypocrisy." No matter that, as Jesus says, "Those who are well have no need of a physician, but those who are sick" (Lk. 5:31), and most of us in the church do not, I hope, consider ourselves particularly "well." Rather we are, individually and collectively, in need of more and more healing.

Some in the world still look on us as the ones who think of themselves as the healed, no longer in need of healing. If that is so, then why not simply witness to the world the power of being an inclusive, healing community, one in which the realities of racism are addressed honestly and real strategies are developed to dismantle these issues within the church itself?

It is clear in some communities that the church, acting to dismantle racist practices in its own life, has in this way been a pioneer in calling other institutions, such as the police, schools, and more, to follow this lead. Kalamazoo, Michigan, for example, has a strong community devoted to anti-racism, and it had early leadership from the church.

Wenatchee, Washington, is another community where the church has been engaged in gathering a collective of community systems, ranging from government (police, schools, social service) to service organizations to learn together a powerful analysis of racism and to develop strategies for dealing with it in their area.

The second area is about the use of authority. Ronald Heifitz and Marty Linsky discuss change as happening in two dimensions, *technical* and *adaptive*. Technical change, they say, is work that addresses problems with already existing "know-how," so that the system already has the method of dealing with the issue at hand. Adaptive change, on the other hand, requires learning new ways of living and facing into the issue. There is no obvious "answer." The people with the problem discern the procedure for dealing with it.[19]

Racism, for the most part, presents adaptive dilemmas. I contend that the answers are not obvious, and they cannot be presented by authority figures. Such matters cannot be fixed by "getting under the hood and taking care of it," as Ross Perot said in his presidential campaign in 1992.

Facing into racism requires leadership that is wise about the limits of its authority, that knows that effective "leadership is not the same as authority,"[20] and that what people fear the most is not change as such, but the loss of what they have. So if people show fear or resistance about what dismantling racism can bring, they need to discover that this is a call to share privilege, not give it up so others can get it. Much of the hue and cry about, for example, affirmative action, is because it is said that this policy will produce advantages for people of color over whites. On the contrary, it is intended to bring us to a place where opportunities and advantages are equally available to all.

Heifitz and Linsky offer one more premise that is important for us to consider. In adaptive work, leadership "requires disturbing people—but at a rate they can absorb."[21] It can be said, then, that leaders exceed the authority given them by enough margin to press change, but at a pace that the community can grasp and come to terms with.

This is the kind of leadership, when coupled with example, that the church can learn how to exert. How do we know it? Because it is the kind of leadership that Jesus exerted and still exerts. We can comb the gospels, and we will find examples of his never asking anything of those who followed that he was not also willing to do (and do first), and of his stepping just beyond what people expected of him in order to offer them a way to walk off the known maps.

Racism can be dismantled with this kind of leadership, and the church can in this way move from being a charitable institution to becoming an agent of community transformation.

Becoming a People of Hope

A lot of people these days have little or no hope of change coming soon in the area of racial transformation. I am not speaking here of eradicating racism totally from what we might call the human "emotional genome." The human family may be trapped for a long time to come by the terrible need of its various tribes, parties, nations, and religions in the dangerous quandary of each one having to find victims, use others, declare ourselves superior, etc.

From the time of the exodus of the Hebrews from slavery in Egypt, being saved has meant to be given a broad place, space, and room to live and grow. *Ye-shua* (the one who leads us to a broad place) was indeed the name of the one who led the Hebrews into Israel, and this is the name that has been anglicized to "Jesus."

If we look at the Christian response to racism through this lens, we see an opportunity to become the church that has, at its heart, the discipline of dismantling racism. In this way we will be guided to claim the space God has already given to countless people. We need to be clear: the ground of our hope is in the belief that *we were created with this space*. It is already there for all of God's children. We can keep others out of God's space only so long and then God's creation will be restored. In reaching this already-given space, those who have privilege and power and those who do not will be saved. The risks of having privilege and power while others do not have it are high. Both those with and those without privilege and power become distorted, wounded, seeing themselves as either far more or far less than God creates us to be. The space God has given us is of a kind in which all share in the privilege of being God's beloved children.

In this way the world will know that we are created to be *one*.

Some Questions for Reflection and Study

1. What is a "movement"? Is it different from a "denomination"? Why or why not?
2. What does it mean to be a "people"?
3. What is the relationship of "prolepsis" to being a spiritual movement?
4. As a people of reason, how do we apply reason in faithful ways to the work of dismantling racism?
5. How do we learn to learn from our mistakes?
6. In what ways is this learning process a spiritual process?
7. What does the gospel say about our response to racism?
8. How can your congregation be a leader in dismantling racism in your community?
9. What basis is there for hope in an effort to dismantle racism?

CHAPTER 10

Your Congregation's Next Steps

If every congregation were to take steps in the effort to confront racism and its evil ways of working, we could make a massive difference in our own movement/denomination, and in the communities where we live and are called to grow.

Whether your congregation is at a point of first or next steps in the struggle to dismantle racism is an important question to address. It is possible to examine this question and thus determine a way to start your collective journey.

Racism's Three Powers—A Tool for Assessment

Racism works in three ways. These are powers with very different levels of force.[1]

The first is racism's power to hurt people of color. It is not the intention of most people who practice racism to kill or even hurt people of color. But historically in the U.S.A. the effect of racism has been to use and abuse massive numbers of people of color. They have been deemed "less than human" for generations, and much of racism's premise and practice has become so "baked into" the very life we live that practices that do harm to people of color continue.

The lowest lying part of New Orleans was relegated years ago to be an African-American community, long a segregated area, and this made it most vulnerable to flooding after Hurricane Katrina. The fact that parents of people of color feel it necessary to caution their children, not about "if" they are stopped by the police, but about "when" they are stopped, points to unjust police practices. Without some assistance (from such initiatives as affirmative action) to "level the playing field," appropriately reflective percentages of enrollments for people of color in colleges and universities will be lower than for whites. All of these realities show that we need not return to the days of slavery, the Chinese Exclusion Act, "sundown" laws in thousands of American towns, or the horrible record of lynching in this land to see the hurting effect of racism. It continues, and as long as racism lives it will have power *over* people of color.

The second is its power to gain power and privilege for white people. This is the foundational reason for racism to begin with, and thus it is a far more powerful reality than the first. If racism's reason for being were simply to hurt certain people, then long ago, we would hope, people of good conscience would have ended it. However, no matter how good the consciences of some white persons, we who are white still gain privilege from racism, and we are conditioned not to think that we are thus privileged.[2] Racism was not invented to harm others but to benefit white persons.

The purpose of slavery was not to demean people, but in the imprisonment and forced enslavements of some 35,000,000 Africans it did this very thing. The intent, though, was to create a labor force. Nor was the breaking of treaties with the American Indian Nations meant to hurt them as much as it was to gain land for white farmers, communities, and industries. That our ancestors didn't feel pangs because of the hurtfulness of their actions is because white persons were already socialized to believe that people of color were less than human, and while it was a shame to hurt them, we could not forgo the benefits or the system. *Racism's third power is its power to destroy all of us, white people and people of color.* Anything that has the force to make some of us think *more of ourselves,* or *less of ourselves,* than we are meant to think—to consider ourselves better or worse than God intends—is destructive. One need only look at the first two powers to see how racism makes people of color see themselves as less and white people see themselves as more. When all of us are created by God to be of equal value, then how can we allow this evil system to distort the creation and make some less and some more? Ultimately this is destruction at its grievous worst.

Our Response to These Powers

If your congregation has already been engaged in addressing racism, what has it done? If it has attempted to alleviate the hurt racism causes but not looked at the reasons the hurt happens to begin with, then it has addressed only the first power. There is nothing wrong with doing this. We must address the many consequences of racism's hurt. Often those who have more will share their gains with those who have less. Many of the victims of Hurricanes Katrina and Rita were people of color, and their need for clothing, shelter, food, medical care, education, and jobs could not be overlooked. There were poignant stories of deep human and pet animal needs to be addressed. Having been to Louisiana in a workweek, I've seen that if people of faith had not responded and were not still responding, the needs would have been even more overwhelming.

We do fool ourselves, however, if we believe that in only addressing the hurts that come from racism we will help eliminate it. Some even say that in *only* responding to racism's hurts white persons and institutions guarantee that they will retain and perpetuate their privilege and power.

If yours is a white or largely white congregation that has also begun to grapple with the benefits whites receive and with ways to undo the system that keeps things this way, then it has started to address the second kind of power. This is far more difficult to do than confronting only the results of racism's hurtfulness. A lot of very brave white persons have been murdered for taking this step (for example, Abraham Lincoln).

Finally, if you have really begun to struggle with the terribly destructive power racism has over all people who are caught up in its sway, white people as well as people of color, then you have begun the difficult journey into racism's third power.

We need to assess our own congregations' responses, including the possibility that our congregations haven't even talked, much less done anything, about this evil.

Possible Steps

Whether your congregation has been mute, responding to racism's first, second, or third power, these steps can be helpful.

Call a leadership group together in the congregation to study this book and other resources in print and media. When this group is ready, identify steps needed to reach to a larger congregational community for interest and support. This group can and probably should include some leaders of the congregation, such as board members and elders. An important element of this group needs to be the level of commitment on the parts of its members. As the congregation's engagement of racism deepens, this group may need to assume a more formal leadership role, because serious work calls for leadership from people who really care that change comes.

Form a partnership team involving persons of more than one race. This can, and most likely should, be related to the above group. We cannot confront racism alone; we need to be in partnership. If you are in a mixed congregation, be sure that the group involves people of color and white people. If yours is a historically white congregation, seek out a congregation of people of color and invite co-equal sharing in this enterprise. *Establish ways to be accountable to people of color.* White people will never confront racism fully until we are willing to be accountable to people of color. Are we accountable? Affirmative action is the one "official" initiative that has dared to say we need to realign the "playing field" for as long as necessary until it is level for people of all races.

Encourage your region/institution to become involved by creating an anti-racism team. Guidance and resources to do this are available from Reconciliation Ministry. If the region already has a team, invite them to do a workshop with people in your congregation, including the leadership group, and then to offer consultative help as you develop strategies to become more engaged in anti-racism work.

Participate in analysis training, offered by Reconciliation Ministry of the Christian Church (Disciples of Christ). This training gives people an understanding of racism's history and power. It will be probable that your congregation's people are not ready for this training until after a year or two of study and reflection. Regional anti-racism leaders can help you plan a sequence of processes that will lead to this training and beyond.

Resources

There are many resources that can be used for the steps you take. There are countless biblical texts, some of which follow:

- Isaiah 40:1–3—A "level" ground for all
- Isaiah 42:1–9—God's passion for justice for all the creation
- Isaiah 61:1–4—God news for *all*
- Amos 5:21–24—Justice and righteousness
- Micah 6:6–8—What God wants of us
- Matthew 25:31–46—God's judgment criteria
- Mark 12:28–34—The most important commandment
- Luke 10:30–37—Who is the real neighbor?
- Acts 10:9–16, 34–43—How big is God's love?

- Acts 17:22–26—God's one creation
- 1 Corinthians 12–13—Being a family of God and love
- Ephesians 2:11–22—Christ is the one who unites

Many other texts from the Bible can be used to discern God's desire and hope for us in the battle against racism's power. We can ask some basic questions about biblical texts:

- Who, why, and what situation was the text about?
- Are there lessons we can learn from that knowledge?
- Are there comparisons of their situation to ours?
- What does the text say about our situation, in particular racism in our time?

Prayer is of absolute importance in the struggle against racism. Whether it is a prayer *asking for insight* about racism's incestuous nature; a *petition,* asking God to help us be faithful in our witness against racism; or an *intercession,* in which we ask God to give strength to those who are engaged in this life-and-death confrontation, prayer needs to be at the center of our work and ministry. Invite your minister to preach about this.

Media can be of great value as TV programs, movies, and Internet resources, for example, are identified. These can be used by your leadership group, other groups, or the congregation as a whole to assess issues of racism. Be sure that quality leadership is provided for such discussions.

Other resources can be seen on the Reconciliation Ministry Web site, to be found through www.disciples.org.

Take Action

Whether it is in providing food for homeless people, offering your building space as housing for the homeless, going to Louisiana or Texas on a work project, or confronting your denominational and outside officials (government or commercial) about policies that obviously or subtly demean people of color, it is important that you take action soon. Discussion and prayer are vital, but they need to lead to action.

Racism doesn't wait for a right and convenient time to do its work. Why, then, should we?

Some Important Things to Remember

The Disciples of Christ are a fertile field for anti-racism work to take place. We have a theological and values history that makes us this. Study chapters 3–8 to see these again. Other core values of our collective life should be added to these. It's important for us to know that our faith in God and our story all add up to ours being a valuable place for this movement to happen.

Prejudice reduction is not the same as anti-racism. While it is important to address individuals' prejudice (and all people have some race prejudice in them) we need to recall that institutional racism goes a step beyond prejudice. It emerges when the race prejudice of people-in-charge is reinforced with the abuse of institutional power. Again and again we see public and private systems carrying out racist policies, not because some individual is prejudiced, but because the collective prejudice of white persons is enforced by the unfair use of that institution's power. It is confronting that abuse of institutional power that is at the soul of anti-racism work

Racism never goes into remission. A close friend who had lymphoma experienced a remission of five years during which his life was normal and he needed minimal treatments. Then, though, it reawakened with a force it had not had before. Within a couple of years he died. Racism, however, never has remission times. It is always alive and working, and as long as this is so it will be as though it is part of the very air we breathe. We can never let down our guard.

Our commitment as a denomination/movement is to become anti-racist by 2030. Will we? The answer depends, I believe, on each congregation's response and, then, willingness to become engaged. I believe that if we are servants of the gospel of Jesus Christ, we have no choice.

Notes

Chapter 1: A Spiritual Movement Begins on the Frontier

[1]Nathan Hatch, *The Democratization of American Christianity* (New Haven, Conn., and London: Yale University Press, 1967), 179.

[2]Barney McLaughlin, at an Arkansas Valley District Assembly workshop, March 1990, Russellville, Ark.

[3]Barton Stone, quoted in William Garrett West, *Barton Warren Stone: Early American Advocate of Christian Unity* (Nashville: The Disciples of Christ Historical Society, 1954), 130.

[4]Mark G. Toulouse, *Joined in Discipleship: The Shaping of Contemporary Disciples Identity* (St. Louis: Chalice Press, 1997), 170.

[5]Ibid., 33–34.

[6]Hoke S. Dickinson, ed., *The Cane Ridge Reader: The Biography of Elder Barton Warren Stone written by himself (and Elder John Rogers)* (Cincinnati: J.A. and U.P. James, 1847), 33–35.

[7]Ibid., 30.

[8]M. Douglas Meeks, *God the Economist* (Minneapolis: Fortress Press, 1989), 88–89.

[9]Howard Zinn, *A People's History of the United States, 1492-Present* (New York: Harper Collins, 2003), 204–5.

[10]Lawrence Cada, Raymond Fitz, Gertrude Foley, Thomas Giardano, and Carol Lichtenberg, *Shaping the Coming Age of Religious Life* (New York: Seabury Press, 1979). This book gives a thorough description of the life cycle of religious organizations, with its primary research being done in the histories of various orders of the Roman Catholic Church.

[11]Meeks, *God the Economist,* 89.

Chapter 2: Born Apart

[1]*Thorndike-Barnhart Student Dictionary* (Glenview, Ill.: Scott, Foresman and Company, 1988), 189.

[2]James Pope-Hennessy, *Sins of the Fathers: The Atlantic Slave Traders 1441-1807* (Edison, N.J.: Castle Books, 1967), 13.

[3]James W. Loewen, *Lies My Teacher Told Me* (New York: Touchstone, 1995), 142.

[4]Robette Ann Dias, *Historical Development of Institutional Racism* (a working paper for Crossroads Antiracism, 2006). Much of the information for the following portion about the historical development of institutional slavery is taken from this paper.

[5]Thomas Jefferson, *Notes on the State of Virginia,* Query XIV, Chapter 14 (*The Writings of Thomas Jefferson: Volume 2,* Electronic Text Center, University of Virginia Library).

[6]Loewen, *Lies My Teacher Told,* 148.

[7]Howard Zinn, *A People's History of the United States, 1492-Present* (New York: Harper Collins, 2003), 129–31.

[8]Ibid., 181.

[9]Paul M. Blowers, "Barclay, James Turner," in *The Encyclopedia of the Stone-Campbell Movement,* ed. Douglas A. Foster, Paul H. Blowers, Anthony L. Dunnavant, D. Newell Williams (Grand Rapids, Mich.: William B. Eerdmans, 2004), 69.

[10]Zinn, *A People's History,* 187.

[11]Vine DeLoria, *Custer Died for Your Sins: An Indian Manifesto* (Norman, Okla.: University of Oklahoma Press, 1969 and 1988), 30–31.

[12]Zinn, *A People's History,* 22–38.

[13]Loewen, *Lies My Teacher Told,* 143.

[14]Ibid., 154. This is a quote in Loewen's work from Paul M. Angle, *Created Equal: The Complete Lincoln-Douglas Debates of 1858* (Chicago: University of Chicago Press, 1958), 22–23.

[15]Don Haymes, Eugene Randall II, and Douglas A. Foster, "Race relations," in *Encyclopedia,* 619.

[16]Ibid., 619.

[17]Ibid., 621–22.

[18]Eva Jean Wrather, *Alexander Campbell: Adventure in Freedom, Volume Two,* ed. D. Duane Cummins (Fort Worth, Tex.: TCU Press and the Disciples of Christ Historical Society, 2007), 320.

[19]Robert Blowers and Robert Fife, "Slavery," in *Encyclopedia,* 685–86.

Chapter 3: Covenantal Values

[1]Letty Russell, *The Future of Partnership* (Louisville: Westminster Press, 1979), 199.

[2]Louis E. Raths, Merrill Harmin, Sidney B. Simon, *Values and Teaching* (Columbus, Ohio: Charles E. Merrell Publishing Co., 1966). The theme of values clarification is discussed in detail throughout this book.

[3]See "Why People Work," available at: http://www.steppingstonesforvets. org/Values/Why_People_Work.pdf.

[4]Raths et al., *Values,* 28–29.

[5]From *The Design of the Christian Church (Disciples of Christ),* obtained from the Office of General Minister and President, Indianapolis, Ind. Available at: http://www.disciples.org/TheDesign.pdf

[6]"He Lives!" *Chalice Hymnal* (St. Louis: Chalice Press, 1995), no. 226.

[7]Jürgen Moltmann, *Theology of Hope* (New York & Evanston: Harper & Row, 1965), 168.

[8]M. Douglas Meeks, *God the Economist* (Minneapolis: Fortress Press, 1989), 88.

[9]Barton Stone, quoted in William Garrett West, *Barton Warren Stone: Early American Advocate of Christian Unity* (Nashville: The Disciples of Christ Historical Society, 1954), 130.

[10]Walter Brueggemann, *Theology of the Old Testament: Testimony, Dispute, Advocacy* (Minneapolis: Fortress Press, 1997), 736.

Chapter 4: I Confess That Jesus Is the Christ

[1]From Robert Browning's poem "Andrea del Sarto," published in 1855.

[2]Robert Cornwall, "Christology," in *The Encyclopedia of the Stone-Campbell Movement,* ed. Douglas A. Foster, Paul H. Blowers, Anthony L. Dunnavant, D. Newell Williams, (Grand Rapids, Mich.: William B. Eerdmans, 2004), 204.

[3]Ibid.

[4]Peter Morgan, "Five Finger Exercise," in *Encyclopedia,* 338.

[5]Ibid., 338–39.

[6]From *The Design of the Christian Church (Disciples of Christ),* obtained from the Office of General Minister and President, Indianapolis, Ind. Available at: http://www.disciples.org/TheDesign.pdf.

[7]Gustavo Gutiérrez, *The God of Life* (Maryknoll, N.Y.: Orbis Books, 1991), 33–34.

[8]Ibid., 34.

⁹The "schwa" is a short vowel sound that occurs only in unstressed syllables. For more information, see Donald H. Ecroyd, Murray M. Halford & Carol Chworowsky Towne, *Voice and Articulation: A Handbook* (Philadelphia: Scott, Foresman and Company, 1966).

¹⁰Letty Russell, *The Future of Partnership* (Louisville: Westminster Press, 1979), 199.

¹¹Ken Anderson, *Dan Moody: Crusader for Justice* (Georgetown, Tex.: Georgetown Press, 2008), 1–2.

Chapter 5: The Open and Inclusive Table

¹D. Newell Williams, "Cane Ridge Revival," in *The Encyclopedia of the Stone-Campbell Movement*, ed. Douglas A. Foster, Paul H. Blowers, Anthony L. Dunnavant, D. Newell Williams (Grand Rapids, Mich.: William B. Eerdmans, 2004), 164–66.

²"Lord's Supper, The," *Encyclopedia*, 490.

³Ibid., 490.

⁴Mark G. Toulouse, *Joined in Discipleship: The Shaping of Contemporary Disciples Identity* (St. Louis: Chalice Press, 1997), 149–50.

⁵Blowers and Lambert, "Lord's Supper, The," 493.

⁶Alexander Campbell, "Communion Affirmation," *Chalice Hymnal* (St. Louis: Chalice Press, 1995), no. 401.

⁷M. Douglas Meeks, *God the Economist* (Minneapolis: Fortress Press, 1989), 88.

Chapter 6: God's Call to All

¹Mark G. Toulouse, *Joined in Discipleship: The Shaping of Contemporary Disciples Identity* (St. Louis: Chalice Press, 1997), 164.

²Ibid., 168.

³Hoke S. Dickinson, ed., *The Cane Ridge Reader: The Biography of Elder Barton Warren Stone written by himself (and Elder John Rogers)* (Cincinnati: J.A. and U.P. James, 1847), 29.

⁴Toulouse, *Joined in Discipleship*, 20.

⁵Ibid., 176. Toulouse quotes here from Alexander Campbell, *The Christian System* (1835), 82.

⁶Leonard Lovett, "Color Lines and the Religion of Racism," in *Ending Racism in the Church*, ed. Susan E. Davies and Sister Paul Teresa Hennessee, S.A., (Cleveland: United Church Press, 1998), 24.

⁷*Constitution of the United States*. It can be found at http://www.constitution.org/constit_.htm.

⁸Paul R. Griffin, *Seeds of Racism in the Soul of America* (Cleveland: Pilgrim Press, 1999), 4–5.

⁹Ibid., 11.

Chapter 7: Our Polar Star

¹Barton Stone, quoted in William Garrett West, *Barton Warren Stone: Early American Advocate of Christian Unity* (Nashville: The Disciples of Christ Historical Society, 1954), 130.

²Hoke S. Dickinson, ed., *The Cane Ridge Reader: The Biography of Elder Barton Warren Stone written by himself (and Elder John Rogers)* (Cincinnati: J.A. and U.P. James, 1847), 79.

³Michael Bollenbaugh, "Reason, place of," in *The Encyclopedia of the Stone-Campbell Movement*, ed. Douglas A. Foster, Paul H. Blowers, Anthony L. Dunnavant, D. Newell Williams (Grand Rapids, Mich.: William B. Eerdmans, 2004), 628.

⁴West, *Barton Warren Stone*, 128.

⁵Barton Stone, quoted in ibid., 119.

⁶Mark G. Toulouse, *Joined in Discipleship: The Shaping of Contemporary Disciples Identity* (St. Louis: Chalice Press, 1997), 53.

⁷Paul Crow Jr., "United Church of Christ–Christian Church (Disciples of Christ) Ecumenical Partnership," in *Encyclopedia*, 754.

⁸Paul R. Griffin, *Seeds of Racism in the Soul of America* (Cleveland: Pilgrim Press, 1999), 17 (quote from the John Winthrop Papers).

⁹Ibid.

¹⁰Ibid., 18.

Chapter 8: Restoring the Justice of God

¹The motion picture *Remember the Titans* was about the football team at T.C. Williams High School in the first year of a very torturous integration. Considering this, the team was something of a miraculous piece of work. It was an excellent team, winning the Virginia 4A state title in 1972.

²Marge Piercy, "A just anger," in *Circles on the Water* (New York: Alfred A. Knopf, 1982), 88 ©1982 by Marge Piercy. Used by permission of Alfred A. Knopf, a division of Random House, Inc.

³Taylor Branch, *Parting the Waters: America in the King Years 1954-62* (New York: Simon & Schuster, 1988); see in particular chapters 8, 9 and 10.

⁴Wikipedia. This reference can be found on http://www.en.wikipedia.org/wiki/Justice delayed is justice denied.htm.

⁵Robette Ann Dias, *Historical Development of Institutional Racism* (a working paper for Crossroads Antiracism, 2006), 20.

⁶William J. Sabol, Todd D. Minton & Paige M. Harrison, *Prison and Jail Inmates at Midyear 2006, Bureau of Justice Statistics Bulletin* (Washington: US. Department of Justice, 2007, revised 03/12/08), 6. Available at: http://www.ojp.usdoj.gov/bjs/pub/pdf/pjim06.pdf.

⁷Ibid.

⁸Mary Elizabeth Hobgood, *Dismantling Privilege: An Ethics of Accountability* (Cleveland: Pilgrim Press, 2000), 23.

⁹Robert Bellah, William M. Sullivan, Ann Swidler, and Steven M. Tipton, *Habits of the Heart* (New York: Harper and Row, 1986), 143.

¹⁰Branch, *Parting the Waters*, 691.

¹¹Jürgen Moltmann, *Theology of Hope* (New York & Evanston: Harper & Row, 1965), 23.

¹²Walter Brueggemann, *Theology of the Old Testament: Testimony, Dispute, Advocacy* (Minneapolis: Fortress Press, 1997), 189, 193.

Chapter 9: Becoming One

¹Ella Mazel, ed., *"And don't call me a racist!": A Treasury of Quotes on the Past, Present and Future of the Color Line in America* (Lexington, Mass.: Argonaut Press, 1998), 8.

²This reference can be found on http://www.en.wikipedia.org/wiki/proleplis.htm.

³James W. Loewen, *Sundown Towns* (New York: The New Press, 2005), 33.

⁴Mary Elizabeth Hobgood, *Dismantling Privilege: An Ethics of Accountability* (Cleveland: Pilgrim Press, 2000), 36.

⁵Peggy McIntosh, "White Privilege: Unpacking the Invisible Knapsack," *Peace and Freedom, a Journal* (July/August 1999). Used with permission of the author.

⁶Ibid.

⁷Audrey Smedley, "Race, the Power of an Illusion," originally available through www.pbs.org.

⁸Walter Brueggemann, *Theology of the Old Testament: Testimony, Dispute, Advocacy* (Minneapolis: Fortress Press, 1997), 193.

⁹George Santayana, "The Life of Reason," quote found at http://en.wikipedia.org/wiki/Santayana.

¹⁰Interview with Rev. Brenda Cardwell, pastor of Pilgrimage Christian Church, Suitland, Md., and coauthor, with William Fox, of *Journey into Discipleship* (December 28, 2007), The National Convocation of the Christian Church (Disciples of Christ).

¹¹Brenda Cardwell, quote from *Old-Timers Grapevine* 16, no. 4 (October-December, 2007).

¹²Audrey Smedley, *Race in North America* (Boulder, Colo.: Westview Press, 1999), 229–40, has an extensive discussion of the scientific manipulation of data to support racial separation theories.

¹³Ibid., 237.

¹⁴James Loewen, *Sundown Towns,* 33.

¹⁵Smedley, *Race in North America,* 240.

¹⁶*Webster's Universal Dictionary and Thesaurus,* 1993.

¹⁷Martin Luther King Jr., quoted in Taylor Branch, *Pillar of Fire: America in the King Years 1963-65* (New York: Simon & Schuster, 1998), 47–48.

¹⁸Ronald Heifitz and Marty Linsky, *Leadership on the Line* (Boston: Harvard Business School Press, 2002), 2.

¹⁹Ibid., 13–14.

²⁰Ibid., 15.

²¹Ibid., 20.

Chapter 10: Your Congregation's Next Steps

¹Adapted from the Analysis of Racism of Crossroads Anti-Racism Organizing and Training, P.O. Box 309, Matteson, IL 60443-0309.

²Peggy McIntosh, "White Privilege: Unpacking the Invisible Knapsack," *Peace and Freedom, a Journal* (July/August 1999).

Bibliography

Anderson, Ken. *Dan Moody—Crusader for Justice.* Georgetown, Tex.: Georgetown Press, 2008.

Bellah, Robert, William M. Sullivan, Ann Swidler, and Steven M. Tipton. *Habits of the Heart.* New York: Harper and Row, 1986.

Branch, Taylor. *Parting the Waters – America in the King Years 1954–62.* New York: Simon & Schuster, 1988.

———. *Pillar of Fire—1963–65.* New York: Simon & Schuster, 1998.

———. *At Canaan's Edge—1965–68.* New York: Simon & Schuster, 2006.

Brueggemann, Walter. *Theology of the Old Testament: Testimony, Dispute, Advocacy.* Minneapolis: Fortress Press, 1997.

Cada, Lawrence, Raymond Fitz, Gertrude Foley, Thomas Giardano, and Carol Lichtenberg. *Shaping the Coming Age of Religious Life.* New York: Seabury Press, 1979.

Davies, Susan E., and Sister Paul Teresa Hennessee, S.A. *Ending Racism in the Church.* Cleveland: United Church Press, 1998.

DeLoria, Vine. *Custer Died for Your Sins, An Indian Manifesto.* Norman, Okla.: University of Oklahoma Press, 1969 and 1988.

Dias, Robette Ann. *Historical Development of Institutional Racism.* A working paper for Crossroads Antiracism, 2006.

Dickinson, Hoke S., ed. *The Cane Ridge Reader: The Biography of Eld. Barton Warren Stone written by himself (and Elder John Rogers).* Cincinnati: J.A. and U.P. James, 1847.

Foster, Douglas A., Paul H. Blowers, Anthony L. Dunnavant, D. Newell, Williams, eds. *The Encyclopedia of the Stone-Campbell Movement.* Grand Rapids., Mich.: William B. Eerdmans, 2004.

Griffin, Paul R. *Seeds of Racism in the Soul of America.* Cleveland: Pilgrim Press, 1999.

Gutiérrez, Gustavo. *The God of Life.* Maryknoll, N.Y.: Orbis Books, 1991.

Hatch, Nathan. *The Democratization of American Christianity.* New Haven, Conn. and London: Yale University Press, 1967.

Heifetz, Ronald, and Marty Linsky. *Leadership on the Line.* Boston: Harvard Business School Press, 2002.

Hobgood, Mary Elizabeth. *Dismantling Privilege, An Ethics of Accountability*. Cleveland: Pilgrim Press, 2000.

Jefferson, Thomas. *Notes on the State of Virginia, Query XIV, Chapter 14*. In *The Writings of Thomas Jefferson*, Volume 2, Electronic Text Center, University of Virginia Library.

Loewen, James W. *Lies My Teacher Told Me*. New York: Touchstone, 1995.

——. *Sundown Towns*. New York, London: The New Press, 2005.

Mazel, Ella, arr. *"And don't call me a racist!" A Treasury of Quotes*. Lexington, Mass.: Argonaut Press, 1998.

McIntosh, Peggy. "White Privilege: Unpacking the Invisible Knapsack," *Peace and Freedom, a Journal* (July/August 1999).

Meeks, M. Douglas. *God the Economist*. Minneapolis: Fortress Press, 1989.

Merrick, Daniel, ed. *Chalice Hymnal*. St. Louis: Chalice Press, 1995.

Moltmann, Jürgen. *Theology of Hope*. New York & Evanston: Harper & Row, 1965.

Pope-Hennessy, James. *Sins of the Fathers – The Atlantic Slave Traders 1441-1807*. Edison, N.J.: Castle Books, 1967.

Raths, Louis E., Merrill Harmin, and Sidney B. Simon. *Values and Teaching*. Columbus, Ohio: Charles E. Merrell Publishing Co., 1966.

Russell, Letty. *The Future of Partnership*. Louisville: Westminster Press, 1979.

Smedley, Audrey. *Race in North America*. Boulder, Colo.: Westview Press, 1999.

——. "Race, the Power of an Illusion," interview originally available through www.pbs.org.

Thorndike-Barnhart Student Dictionary. Glenview, Ill.: Scott, Foresman and Co., 1988.

Toulouse, Mark G. *Joined In Discipleship: the Shaping of Contemporary Disciples Identity*. St. Louis: Chalice Press, 1997.

West, William Garrett. *Barton Warren Stone: Early American Advocate of Christian Unity*. Nashville: The Disciples of Christ Historical Society, 1954.

Wrather, Eva Jean, *Alexander Campbell – Adventure in Freedom, Volume Two*. Edited by D. Duane Cummins. Ft. Worth, Tex.: TCU Press and the Disciples of Christ Historical Society, 2007.

Zinn, Howard. *A People's History of the United States 1492-Present*. New York: HarperCollins, 2003.